ADVANCE PRAISE

"Wise and revolutionary. These are skilled and caring teachers giving you the real deal. They have learned how work with adolescent energy and show how to foster a genuine sense of belonging, and how to soothe, inspire, and awaken the teenage spirit."
— Jack Kornfield, Ph.D., bestselling author of *A Path with Heart*

"Bolstered by the authors' years of meditation practice and real-world experience, *Teaching Mindfulness to Empower Adolescents* is an invaluable resource for anyone who practices mindfulness and meditation with teens. At its core, this excellent book is a tract on how to navigate the ups and downs of daily life that not only supports readers in their work with adolescents but in their own lives as well."
— Susan Kaiser Greenland, author of *The Mindful Child*, *Mindful Games*, and the Inner Kids Program

"In a time when teens face real inner and outer challenges, and quick-fix, faux mindfulness offerings are increasingly popular, this book is a true gift. Every page is infused with the authors' deep personal mindfulness practices and their years of experience in sharing these practices with diverse youth. The authors recognize that sharing mindfulness with young people is profound and transformative, and that collaborative mindful action is required to address the systemic issues that are causing our youth to suffer. This book is a powerful and heartfelt contribution to the field, and an essential read for those committed to offering mindfulness with integrity and authenticity."
— Amy Saltzman, M.D., Director of Still Quiet Place, Director of the Association for Mindfulness in Education

"*Teaching Mindfulness to Empower Adolescents* is a gorgeous gift in learning how to raise a generation of empaths. I am so grateful for the lesson in 'building relationships, leaving space, and establishing personal relevance.' As a parent and individual, I felt deep support and a renewed understanding in the most important teachings and practices a person can have. I particularly loved this book's guidance on the reminder to 'make space to listen.' Thank you to JoAnna Hardy, Matthew Brensilver, and Oren Jay Sofer for bringing such essential teaching to light."
— Laura Dern, Actor and Producer

"In a world with many wonderful books on an important topic, this one stands above the crowd with practical advice built on hard won experience. I've been waiting for these excellent teachers to write up their wisdom, and they've exceeded my high expectations. Organized effectively and written in straightforward language, in this book Brensilver, Hardy, and Sofer empower not just adolescents but their caregivers and communities as well. A gift to mindfulness educators everywhere."

— Christopher Willard, Psy.D., author of *Growing Up Mindful* and *Alphabreaths*, part time faculty at Harvard Medical School

"In teaching mindfulness to adolescents, the 'what' (curriculum) is important, but not as important as the 'how' (quality of the teacher's presence and mindset). This book shows the way to give life to mindfulness teaching with authenticity, ethics, and integrity—always starting with, and coming back to, the teacher's own personal mindfulness practice. I highly recommended it to all adults who wants to bring mindfulness to youth, and to all adults who care deeply about young people."

— Dzung X. Vo, M.D., author of *The Mindful Teen: Powerful Skills to Help You Handle Stress One Moment at a Time*

"This book is a cutting-edge resource for any youth professional wanting to share mindfulness with teens. Brensilver, Hardy, and Sofer offer a skillful, innovative, and developmentally tailored approach that promotes youth receptivity and buy-in. Sharing mindfulness is much more than teaching techniques, and this book will give you everything you need; from the practice of cultivating relationships, to working with resistance, to tough conversations about the issues teens struggle with. I recommend this book without hesitation."

— Sam Himelstein, Ph.D., author of *Trauma-Informed Mindfulness with Teens: A Guide for Mental Health Professionals*

Teaching Mindfulness to Empower Adolescents

Teaching Mindfulness to Empower Adolescents

Matthew Brensilver | JoAnna Hardy | Oren Jay Sofer

W. W. NORTON & COMPANY

Independent Publishers Since 1923

For information about permission to reproduce selections from this book, write to
Permissions, W. W. Norton & Company, Inc., 500 Fifth Avenue, New York, NY 10110

For information about special discounts for bulk purchases, please contact
W. W. Norton Special Sales at specialsales@wwnorton.com or 800-233-4830

Manufacturing by Sheridan Books
Production manager: Katelyn MacKenzie

Library of Congress Cataloging-in-Publication Data

Names: Brensilver, Matthew, author. | Hardy, JoAnna (Meditation practitioner), author. | Sofer,
    Oren Jay, author.
Title: Teaching mindfulness to empower adolescents / Matthew Brensilver, JoAnna Hardy, and
    Oren Jay Sofer.
Description: First edition. | New York : W.W. Norton & Company, 2020. | Series: Norton
    books in education | Includes bibliographical references and index.
Identifiers: LCCN 2019030055 | ISBN 9780393713794 (paperback) | ISBN
    9780393713800 (epub)
Subjects: LCSH: Attention--Study and teaching. | Mindfulness (Psychology)—Study and
    teaching. | Reflective learning. | Teaching—Aids and devices.
Classification: LCC BF321 .B8185 2020 | DDC 155.5/1913071—dc23
LC record available at https://lccn.loc.gov/2019030055

W. W. Norton & Company, Inc., 500 Fifth Avenue, New York, N.Y. 10110
www.wwnorton.com

W. W. Norton & Company Ltd., 15 Carlisle Street, London W1D 3BS

1 2 3 4 5 6 7 8 9 0

To Jeff, Joanne, and Greg, for weathering my adolescence.

—

Matthew

To all of the young people who trusted my guidance and shared their beautiful hearts and minds with me over the past twenty years. And to CJ, Harris, and Andre for your unwavering love, laughter, kindness, and support.

—

JoAnna

For the young adults and adolescents who are struggling to find their way in a world on fire. And for the parents, teachers, and educators who are working to support young people. May we find the humility, love, and wisdom to learn from each other.

—

Oren

CONTENTS

Acknowledgments   xiii

Introduction   xv

CHAPTER 1

The Promise of Mindfulness   1

CHAPTER 2

Tailoring Mindfulness
to Adolescent Development   15

CHAPTER 3

You Are the Instrument:
Personal Practice and Embodied Teaching   29

CHAPTER 4

Mutual Respect:
Creating Connection and Building Relationship   53

CHAPTER 5

Establishing Relevance and Fostering
Group Engagement   75

CHAPTER 6

Working with Resistance and Overcoming Obstacles   95

CHAPTER 7

Anger, Self-Harshness,
and Self-Compassion   115

CHAPTER 8

Navigating Pleasures and Distractions:
Technology, Sex, and Substances   137

CHAPTER 9

Trauma, Mindfulness, and Mitigating Harm   153

CHAPTER 10

Our Moment: Expanding the Circle of Care   171

References   185

Further Resources   195

Index   201

ACKNOWLEDGMENTS

This book owes a great debt to the contributions of two people in the wider field of mindfulness in education: Megan Cowan and Chris McKenna. Megan cofounded Mindful Schools, developing the first version of its mindfulness curriculum and piloting the program in the schools of Oakland, California. She was later joined at Mindful Schools by Program Director Chris McKenna, who brought his expertise in curriculum development, organizational management, and trauma-informed mindfulness practice. Together, Megan and Chris inspired thousands of educators around the world to learn, practice, and share mindfulness in schools. For years, we have worked closely with Megan and Chris and two other beloved colleagues, Pam Dunn and Vinny Ferraro. Though their names appear infrequently in the text, the imprint of their ideas is intimately woven throughout these pages.

We also wish to express our deep gratitude to the educators, counselors, and facilitators sharing mindfulness with youth every day in schools, agencies, and programs. In particular, we would like to thank the following individuals for their generosity in offering their expertise and stories through interviews that we conducted for this book: Khalila Gillett Archer, Enrique Collazo, Morris Ervin, Forest Fein, Jozen Tamori Gibson, Jessica Morey, Charisse Minerva, Dave Smith, Jaylin Speight, Bart van Melik, and Doug Worthen.

We would like to thank our own meditation teachers and mentors. Without their transmission and guidance, we would lack the practice and understanding that allow us to teach young people and write from our own experience: Ajahn Sucitto, Diana Winston, Gil Fronsdal, Godwin Samararatne, Jack Kornfield, Joseph Goldstein, Kittisaro, Marvin Belzer, Michele McDonald, Shinzen Young, Shri Natha Devi, and Thanissara.

Finally, this book would not be possible without the young people each of us has had the privilege of knowing. As we share in these pages, we learn as much from them as they learn from us. Our hope is that this book benefits their learning, growth and future.

INTRODUCTION

Think back to your adolescence. What did you want most from the adults around you? How did you want to be treated? What conversations did you long to be having, but could not? We view mindfulness less as a technique and more as a deeply honest conversation with ourselves and with each other. It is a conversation that includes all of the joy and sorrow, love and loss that constitutes a human life.

As adults, we can facilitate this radical honesty within and among adolescents. When we sit together in a room with young people, we silently express our abiding wish that they might be happy. As we look around at their faces, the power and potential of their lives is palpable. It's a privilege to spend time with young people and see the light inside go on when they discover the landscape of their minds and sense the freedom that comes from self-understanding.

We sit with them, aware of our shared goodness and our shared imperfection. We hope to help them grow and are willing to be changed by them. In this willingness, they can sense our care.

How can we as educators, as parents, and as caring adults support adolescents to understand themselves and transform the world they are inheriting? How can we uncover their innate gifts and passions in a society that is often dismissive of their voices? Harnessing the potentials of adolescence requires that we reexamine this stage of human life and provide more support for empowering their voices.

Although adolescence is often caricatured as a phase of self-absorption, it is also a time when altruistic concerns become urgent and sensitivity to fairness is heightened (Bryan et al., 2016).

It's not surprising that adolescents, unburdened by the dogmas of a previous generation, agitate for social change and influence the evolution of societal norms. Young people push the boundaries of the status quo and challenge adults to grow, learn, and adapt. Whether it's the swell of youth support for the Black Lives Matter movement, students who have been targets of school violence organizing for gun control, teens challenging traditional gender roles, or Greta Thunberg addressing members the UN Climate Change Conference and being catapulted into a role of world leadership, adolescents are demanding a voice in the conversation about the direction of our society.

Our society is often structured to meet the needs of adults, forcing children to conform to an adult world, rather than working to discover what children need to learn, grow, and contribute in meaningful ways. One can see this on a daily basis in the simplest of interactions: young children are routinely discouraged from crying or expressing emotion, and this is to meet adults' needs for ease or efficiency. Witness the immediate stress and embarrassment of a parent in a public place when their child begins crying or misbehaving— acting like a child instead of a miniature adult. In many schools, children are required to study the same subjects in the same ways regardless of differences in learning styles and interest. Even the modern phenomenon of so-called helicopter parenting, in which parents become overly obsessed with a child's needs, can be understood as a response to our culture's emphasis on material success, which places extraordinary pressure and unrealistic expectations on parents to maximize their children's achievement. This is evidenced in the recent scandal about parents who are accused of paying hundreds of thousands of dollars in bribes to get their children admitted to prestigious universities.

We believe that education is about more than transmitting information and that mindfulness can play a key role in the healthy maturation of teens and young adults. Mindfulness is a valuable life skill and a key developmental ingredient. Perhaps even more, self-awareness is a right. As Socrates once said over 2000 years ago (while on trial in part for "corrupting youth" with his ideas), "The unexamined life is not worth living." Introspection is a gateway to self-discovery, understanding, and fulfillment.

A human life is more than a collection of experiences, more than a series of moments and relationships. There is something mysterious, perhaps ineffable about being alive. One of our deepest needs as human beings—together with needs for love, connection, belonging, and contribution—is the need for meaning. While mindfulness practice itself takes no particular stance on what we might call this spiritual dimension of human existence, we see the development of awareness as a key support for maturing as human beings and growing in this domain.

In these pages, we share a range of perspectives, tools, and stories that we hope will inspire you to develop deeper relationships with the young people in your lives and guide you to collaborate with them to build a better world. We'll include stories of adolescents whose lives have been shifted in small or dramatic ways by the practice. Although this book is about teaching mindfulness to adolescents, its broader hope is that mindfulness becomes a vehicle for honoring the dignity and wisdom of the developmental phase. At the heart of mindfulness practice is developing an authentic relationship with oneself and with other human beings.

We have seen through our own experience, and through the experiences of thousands of students and educators, that mindfulness is a transformative practice to support these ends. At the same time, many of the principles we share can also be applied to empowering youth in a range of other contexts: mentoring, sports, music, yoga, therapy, and other modalities of healing, education, and personal development. We hope that you will take the ideas and information in these pages and make good use of them to support, encourage, and empower the youth in your life.

Teaching Mindfulness
to Empower
Adolescents

CHAPTER 1

THE PROMISE OF MINDFULNESS

She sat in rapt attention, as if listening to the story of how her own life might unfold. After the weekly session had ended, the young woman came to discuss her experience with the instructor. With tears in her eyes, she confessed that until she began practicing mindfulness, she didn't believe it was possible to be happy. Now, she said, she understood something new about herself and the potential of her own heart.

DRAMATIC MOMENTS SUCH AS THIS ONE ARE DEEPLY poignant, and they are not uncommon in mindfulness training. Some adolescents quickly sense the transformative potential of mindfulness. Since Jon Kabat-Zinn's groundbreaking work in the 1980s with chronic pain patients in a basement room at University of Massachusetts Medical Center, mindfulness has spread through the fields of health care, mental health, education, and beyond. In the last 25 years, the rise of mindfulness-based applications in medicine (Ludwig & Kabat-Zinn, 2008) psychology (Kuyken et al., 2016), and education (Roeser, Skinner, Beers & Jennings, 2012), have catapulted mindfulness into public consciousness as an accessible tool for stress reduction, performance enhancement, healing, and personal transformation. There is burgeoning interest in integrating mindfulness into the lives of youth in education and mental health treatment. The United Kingdom even has a parliamentary work group that is developing recommendations for integrating mindfulness in education, health, workplace, and criminal justice settings.

WHAT IS MINDFULNESS?

In spite of its growing popularity, the quality of mindfulness itself and the practices that support its cultivation are often misunderstood. It is regularly reduced to an attention-focusing technique and commonly categorized as merely another self-help tool to manage stress or feel calmer. While mindfulness practice includes training to stabilize our attention, and while it often results in stress reduction and increased states of well-being, it involves much more.

Mindfulness practice as we know it today in the West has its roots in and is derived from the ancient tradition of Buddhist meditation. Many of the techniques and practices that are taught throughout the world today originated within the context of Buddhist monastics seeking to understand and transform consciousness.

Yet the capacity for mindfulness itself is not religious, nor need one ascribe to any set of beliefs to explore the techniques that develop it. Mindfulness is an innate mental quality that all humans possess. Jon Kabat-Zinn (2003), who developed the 8-week program known as Mindfulness-Based Stress Reduction (MBSR), defines mindfulness as, "The awareness that emerges from paying attention on purpose, in the present moment, and non-judgmentally to the unfolding of experience" (p. 145). Put more succinctly, it is the capacity to be aware in a balanced, open, and nonreactive way. The practices that support its cultivation are entirely secular. They require no adherence to any particular doctrine, dogma, or worldview; they do not assert the notion that certain texts or ideas have special, sacred, or protected status; they are evidence-based and open to revision as new data emerge from the scientific community.

As the word *mindfulness* becomes more ubiquitous, there is risk that its meaning will be diluted. While no single individual or group is empowered to determine the final meaning of mindfulness, a consensual definition will ultimately emerge out of the ongoing conversation among practitioners, scholars, and scientists. Indeed, an individual's own understanding of mindfulness evolves dramatically over the course of practice; in a way, mindfulness is only understood through the result of practice. That said, beginning with conceptual clarity can support one in the journey to a more direct, personal understanding. There are different models to understand mindfulness and different ways to define it. Here, we'll present a few different perspectives with the aim that examining mindfulness from multiple angles will present a fuller picture of what it encompasses.

The word mindfulness gets used in at least three ways: as a state, a trait, and a practice. We can have a moment of mindfulness (state) and also have a habitual tendency of mindfulness (trait). We can intentionally and formally undertake the development of mindfulness (practice) using different mental training exercises, postures, and activities: for example, seated mindfulness, breath awareness, or mindful walking. These formal *practices* of mindfulness lead to more moments of the *state* of mindfulness and ultimately improved *trait-level* mindfulness. Higher trait-level mindfulness means that we're more mindful even when we're not consciously trying to be mindful. This is important: we're learning to create a healthy habit of mindfulness.

Another common way of understanding mindfulness is through the two key factors that it comprises: present-moment awareness and equanimity, a balanced nonreactivity. The combination of these two factors are what gives mindfulness its potency.

Present-moment awareness is the direct, clear, subjective knowing of experience. This awareness is not merely cognitive. It is not about *disconnecting* from what's happening and observing it from a remote standpoint. It entails an embodied and affective awareness. To be mindful means to be intimate with experience, to live in our own skin here and now, feeling the nuances of what it is to be alive at this particular moment. In mindful awareness, there is a felt sense, an embodied awareness of our physical existence, and the ability to feel fully the richness of our emotional life. To be mindful of sound is to hear completely and directly. To be mindful of an emotion is to feel fully and deeply. To be intimate with experience is different from being entangled with it. Equanimity allows us to connect with experience without becoming lost in it. → choice

Equanimity is cognitive and emotional balance, a steady, inner poise that gives us the space to refrain from acting out our preferences. It connotes ease, nonreactivity, and nonmanipulation. Equanimity represents a balance between suppressing experience on the one hand and getting entangled with experience on the other. The balance that is equanimity gives us the space to feel and sense what's happening without getting lost in or overwhelmed by it. This nonreactivity supports healing, develops resilience, and confers choice.

The capacity of nonreactivity also allows us to us to stay conscious of a sensation, thought, emotion, or impulse long enough to observe its ephemeral nature without immediately reacting. In formal, seated meditation, when one experiences a strong itching sensation or the urge to stand up and end the session, if there is enough equanimity one can observe that sensation or impulse long enough to see it change. Equanimity gives us the ability to tolerate that experience appearing, growing more intense, and then weakening and eventually disappearing. This skill has direct benefits in our day-to-day life, where equanimity supports us to feel an emotion like frustration or anger without needing to make a sharp comment or snap at someone. For teens and adolescents, as equanimity grows with mindfulness practice, their ability to find more balance with challenging moods and emotions increases.

Sometimes, equanimity is confused with indifference, detachment, or passive acceptance of suffering in the world. This is a complete misunderstanding. Equanimity is a *momentary acceptance* that marks our relation to present-time experience, not our relation to objective conditions in the world. We can be nonreactive to our present-moment, subjective experience, while still being deeply committed to changing and improving the conditions in the world.

Another important part of comprehending mindfulness practice is understanding a host of related mental qualities that support (and are supported by) its development, qualities like concentration, persistence, and positive states such as kindness. Concentration is a gathered and stable quality of the mind whereby the attention is unified and stays focused on a chosen object of awareness. This attentional stability has a range of benefits and real-life applications: from learning readiness and academic achievement to nondistracted pursuit of goals. The combination of mindfulness (balanced, nonreactive awareness) and concentration (staying power) supports both contemplative investigation as well as a richer experience of well-being in life.

Mindfulness also entails a relaxed, persistent effort. It contains within it the ability to *remember* to pay attention in this particular way, moment after moment. Thus, each moment of mindful awareness creates the conditions for the next moment of mindfulness. The more mindful we are, the more likely we are to continue to be mindful.

CONSIDER THIS . . .

*For once, we get to not **do** anything, to not **be** anybody, to not go anywhere. Celebrate the absence of doing and the invitation to truly rest.*

The practice of mindfulness is often paired with a suite of associated techniques for cultivating positive mind states like gratitude, kindness and forgiveness. In these practices, one uses mindfulness as the basis to apply attention to a particular prosocial emotion, enhancing and strengthening access to that emotion through specific, repeated exercises and techniques. Often referred to as *heart practices*, these prosocial emotions deepen relationships, provide robust soft skills for personal and professional endeavors, and further enhance one's quality of life.

MINDFULNESS AND SOCIAL AND EMOTIONAL LEARNING: OVERLAPS AND DIFFERENCES

Mindfulness is relatively new to education, and many school leaders want more clarity about how mindfulness fits with another recent initiative in many schools and districts, social and emotional learning or SEL. Should principals and superintendents be choosing between these approaches, or using both? There are important overlaps between mindfulness and SEL, yet they are sufficiently different that they can work well in concert, each complementing the other. Let's look more closely at the practices, skills, and outcomes of mindfulness and SEL.

Skills and Practices: Mindfulness

In one prominent model of mindfulness, Michael Posner and colleagues (Tang, Hölzel, & Posner, 2015) suggested that mindfulness contains three core skill sets: attentional control, emotion regulation, and self-awareness. All mindfulness training includes activities and exercises to help with the intentional development of particular skills and outcomes, including:

+ *Attentional Control:* Students learn to sustain the attention, detect mind-wandering, and return the attention to the chosen object when they become entangled in discursive thought.
+ *Emotion Regulation:* Students engage in activities designed to develop flexibility in navigating emotional experience such that they can optimally pursue valued goals.
+ *Self-awareness:* Mindfulness confers its benefits through the development of self-awareness skills. Self-awareness includes present-moment awareness of somatic and emotional cues. It also refers to decreases in self-referential thinking and increases in flexibility in the ideas we have about ourselves.

As a practice and approach to living, mindfulness aims at profound flourishing. Practiced over a period of years, mindfulness seeks to create an emotionally balanced, meaningful life, animated by a spirit of compassion and caring.

CONSIDER THIS . . .

The fruit of mindfulness is often seen in retrospect. It's like looking in a rear-view mirror—we begin to notice what we're not doing anymore, how we're not obsessing, how we're not doing that annoying thing, how we didn't make a poor choice.

Skills and Practices: Social and Emotional Learning

Let us consider the practices, skills, and outcomes of social and emotional learning models. The Collaborative for Academic, Social, and Emotional Learning (CASEL), the leading organization in disseminating high-quality SEL programming, highlights five core SEL *skills* including self-awareness, self-management, social awareness, relationship skills, and responsible decision making. Self-management and self-awareness are skills practiced internally, social awareness and relationship skills are, of course, interpersonal, and responsible decision making is practiced both internally and interpersonally.

+ *Self-Awareness:* Recognition of one's inner experience and how it influences behavior.
+ *Self-Management:* Regulation of one's emotions, thoughts, and behavior, including the management of stress and the ability to pursue goals in a coherent manner.
+ *Social Awareness:* The ability to empathize and understand the inner lives of others from one's own or other cultural backgrounds.

- *Relationship Skills:* The ability to establish and maintain healthy relationships.
- *Responsible Decision Making:* The ability to make positive choices about personal behavior and social interactions.

In an important review of more than 270,000 students receiving SEL programming (Durlak, Weissberg, Dymnicki, Taylor & Schellinger, 2011), researchers highlighted five key outcomes of SEL programs:

1. Healthy attitudes
2. Positive social behavior
3. Reduced substance use
4. Reduced emotional distress
5. Improved academic performance (p. 407)

The researchers found that school-wide SEL programs, delivered by classroom teachers, demonstrated benefits in all five key outcomes. These benefits were considered small but meaningful. Of special interest, academic performance was improved by 11%, which is larger than the average effect of a typical academic-focused intervention.

Divergences and Synergy Between Mindfulness and Social and Emotional Learning

Clearly, there is substantial overlap between the practices, skills, and outcomes targeted by mindfulness and SEL programs. Bear in mind that many mindfulness programs implicitly or explicitly incorporate aspects of SEL, and SEL programs sometimes involve small doses of training in mindfulness practices.

At the same time, there are certain differences between these approaches. The practices of SEL rely more heavily on psychoeducation and interpersonal skill development. Although mindfulness may include some similar exercises, mindfulness functions more centrally as intrapersonal attention and emotion training. Mindfulness more closely resembles training such as physical exercise. In mindfulness practice—as in exercise—there is less emphasis on cognitive understanding and more emphasis on engaging the mind-body in particular ways. While the skills of the approaches have considerable overlap, SEL more explicitly focuses on creating harmonious classrooms and communities. Mindfulness invests heavily in developing self-regulation. SEL includes self-regulation but emphasizes interpersonal and decision-making skills. When students self-regulate more effectively due to mindfulness, we expect their relationships to improve. However, mindfulness does not typically target relationship skills in the same explicit manner SEL does.

Comparing the target outcomes of mindfulness and SEL, again, we find overlap and notable differences. Mindfulness is often less explicitly goal-oriented. Of course, in order to conduct research and introduce mindfulness in education, mindfulness programs need to specify targeted outcomes. Nevertheless, explicit emphasis on particular desired outcomes can undermine the unpressured, investigatory spirit of the practice. SEL more clearly specifies the desired outcomes: prosocial behavior, emotion regulation, and academic performance. SEL is also more likely to specify long-term outcomes regarding success in adulthood.

So, how might mindfulness and SEL programming support each other? When experts develop, test, and disseminate a program—mindfulness, SEL, or another—it is not uncommon to develop deep personal investments in one's own particular approach. Additionally, program developers regularly compete for limited resources: funding, classroom time, teacher energy, and leadership support. These factors can create a zero-sum game, where a win for one program is considered a loss for another. We hope that mindfulness and SEL can transcend this dynamic and that the most effective elements of each approach can be incorporated and leveraged for greatest benefit.

What value might mindfulness add to existing SEL programs? By targeting the three key skills of attentional control, emotion regulation, and self-awareness, mindfulness builds student self-regulation to a greater extent than do SEL programs alone. In turn, self-regulation allows students to think clearly enough to utilize strategies they learned in their social and emotional learning curriculum. We frequently hear from educators that mindfulness provides a missing piece of awareness and self-regulation that facilitates using SEL strategies most effectively. Second, the attention-training aspect of mindfulness is likely to be relevant for academic achievement and learning SEL skills. Mindfulness decreases mind-wandering, which is associated with poorer task performance. Experimental evidence suggests that enhanced attention can improve reading comprehension and cognitive capacities. Last, mindfulness may be beneficial in promoting the prosocial attitudes and behavior that form a centerpiece of SEL. The classic description of empathy—to stand in someone else's shoes—presumes that we already know what it is like to stand in our own shoes. With striking clarity, mindfulness reveals what it's like to experience difficult as well as pleasant emotions. The intimacy of our encounter with ourselves provides a deeper basis for accurate empathy.

As the dialogue between these two modalities continues to unfold, we believe there is much to be gained from implementing these approaches side by side or finding ways to integrate them synergistically. The practices, skills, and outcomes of mindfulness and SEL are largely complementary. Their commonalities make them good partners, while their differentiation suggests that one approach can profitably be integrated with the other.

THE PLACE OF MINDFULNESS IN EDUCATION

The surge of interest in mindfulness among educators testifies not only to the altruistic wish to benefit one's students, but also to the possibility of recapturing the humanistic bond that characterizes the best student-teacher relationships. As the pressures and priorities of the education system have evolved, some educators say that the sanctity of the relationship with students has eroded. Mindfulness represents an opportunity to restore the affective connection between teacher and student that many crave.

The word *education* comes from the Latin *educare*, which means *to lead forth*. To lead adolescents requires a relationship: a dynamic exchange of words, gestures, and care. We are gently inviting someone, drawing the person onwards, rather than forcing or demanding. True education puts the learner at the center, and aims to awaken the person's full humanity.

We believe that a complete education must include exploration of the mind and heart—of our inner life. For this, mindfulness is an invaluable skill, essential for both adolescent development and adult thriving. Mindfulness practice reveals our inner world, provides a tool to explore it, and develops skills to exercise agency with the tides of emotion and swells of thought that can dominate our lives. For many teens and young adults who learn mindfulness practice, it is how they first become cognizant of their inner life.

One high school senior participating in a mindfulness course shared how the practice helped her begin to feel and process her feelings of heartbreak over the fact that her mom had left home a few years ago. Until the course, she'd been feeling depressed, apathetic, and down on herself. Through the practice, she learned to differentiate between her actual emotions and the beliefs she'd formed to protect herself from the pain—beliefs like "there's something wrong with me . . . she never loved me . . . I can't trust people." She saw that the thoughts weren't necessarily true, but were an expression of her deep pain. For teens and adolescents, whose sense of self and identity are undergoing rapid changes, distinguishing their actual experience from the stories in their mind is paramount. Separating a feeling from rumination and emotional proliferation is the beginning of inner freedom.

As the inner life is revealed, the capacity for (and benefits of) nonreactivity become clearer. At one 6-day mindfulness retreat for adolescents held near San Jose, California, there was a scare about an outbreak of bed bugs. Over a period of 24 hours, a flurry of activity ensued as the staff figured out how to take the necessary health precautions over New Year's Eve, when typical professional services were unavailable. In the midst of a complex and stressful process, with over 50 people running clothes through a high-heat commercial dryer and bagging all other clothing to be decontaminated, one of the adolescents approached the staff. He said, "This is why we've been practicing all this week. It's for challenging moments like this. But it's so easy to forget our mindfulness. It's like we're in water and we forget and we're trying to breath air. But we can remember."

Aspirations for a more holistic education that awakens youth to the fullness of their humanity are often in conflict with the pressures and demands of public education. Although the rewards of teaching can be profound, educators face job stresses that challenge the maintenance of emotional balance. Teachers are charged with creating a structured learning environment that promotes academic achievement, intellectual curiosity, and socioemotional development. Accountability to standardized learning outcomes intensifies the demands of teaching. Successfully meeting these objectives places a significant burden on teachers. Unsurprisingly, more than 50% of teachers rate their work as very stressful. Forty percent of teachers leave the profession within the first 5 years of teaching and high rates of early retirement exist. These trends testify to the rigors of the profession.

Mindfulness cannot answer all these needs. In fact, attempting to make mindfulness a panacea is a sure way to distort the practice. We recognize the pressing need for structural changes in the education system and are in no way suggesting that mindfulness should be a silver bullet self-help strategy for educators to resolve burnout and stress. This parallels a critique within medicine and research on physician burnout, where some have argued that offering self-care strategies for providers unfairly shifts the responsibility from institutions to individuals. Indeed, systemic approaches are needed to rebalance the life of the educator. Nevertheless, we hold substantial hope that mindfulness practice can provide support for educators to manage the stress of working in a high-pressure environment while helping to ensure the dignity of the student-teacher relationship. Although the research is preliminary, educators practicing mindfulness report increased job satisfaction and lower stress (Roeser et al., 2012). Healthier adults, who are less stressed and more self-aware, are more emotionally available to support adolescent development.

CHAPTER 2

TAILORING MINDFULNESS TO ADOLESCENT DEVELOPMENT

There is a familiar rhythm to the academic year in a university setting. In late summer, the minivans roll up and the first-year students begin arriving. They appear with their luggage, posters, and parents, with their earnestness and their fear. The ubiquitous concern about social standing is palpable. You can almost smell the need to belong and the fear of exclusion. The students perform their identities with such ardor—dressing, speaking, and behaving with great care. They curate their identities with exquisite attunement to the social pressures of the moment.

AS A GRADUATE STUDENT AND THEN RESEARCHER at universities for over a decade, Matthew found it poignant to watch this process, the vulnerability of the spectacle, students' hearts ascending or descending according to social standing. It reminds us of our own social sensitivity and of our common human developmental history. While we never become fully immune to the pressures of being 18 years old, our recollection as adults of the acute sensitivities of that phase of life are often muted. The more we are able to remember, understand, and appreciate how it actually feels to be an adolescent—the intensity of the emotions, the tangle of thoughts, and swell of impulses—the better we are able to share mindfulness with adolescent students in ways that are relevant and effective.

If adolescents don't understand *why* they're practicing mindfulness, we cannot expect sincere effort and engagement. Teaching mindfulness to adolescents can't be a simple downward extension of mindfulness for adults. To make mindfulness relevant to adolescents requires tailoring it specifically to their developmental phase. Mindfulness must speak directly to the key existential preoccupations of adolescents. If we ignore their unique concerns and developmental tasks, programming falls flat. In this chapter, we'll consider the salient features of adolescent development and explore how these can inform our mindfulness teaching.

A CRUCIAL PERIOD OF DEVELOPMENT

The journalist Earl Wilson once remarked that "Snow and adolescence are the only problems that disappear if ignored for long enough" ("Adolescence research," 2018). That's a good line, and anyone who works with adolescents can probably sympathize with the sentiment. But, of course, it's also wrong! In a report titled "Our Future," a leading medical journal, *The Lancet*, highlighted the crucial importance of addressing the needs of 1.8 billion adolescents around the globe:

> Firstly, health and wellbeing underpin the crucial developmental tasks of adolescence including the acquisition of the emotional and cognitive abilities for independence, completion of education and transition to employment, civic engagement, and formation of lifelong relationships. Secondly, adolescence and young adulthood can be seen as the years for laying down the foundations for health that determine health trajectories across the life course. Lastly, adolescents are the next generation to parent; these same health reserves do much to determine the healthy start to life they provide for their children. (Patton et al., 2016, p. 2426)

Until recently, scientific research and governmental policy had largely overlooked adolescence in favor of infancy, childhood, and adulthood. We now know that during adolescence the brain undergoes a particularly dynamic period of development; only in infancy are the neurobiological changes of similar significance and magnitude. As the eminent pediatrician Ronald Dahl (2018) explains, the "diverse changes across brain systems in adolescence result in a series of shifts in how the brain attends to, integrates and retains information. This means that changes in the brain during adolescence not only shape behavior, but also learning—in ways that could have a lifelong impact" (p. 443).

The heightened malleability of adolescent brain development highlights the importance of our work to create supportive environments and guide adolescents through this important phase. The social, emotional, and educational resources they accrue (or miss) during this time can have enduring effects over a lifetime. If we want to support kids, create healthy adults, and, by extension, engender a thriving society, we need to invest in interventions that enhance resilience and promote flourishing in adolescents. Interventions that support socioemotional growth during adolescence may have the potential to minimize or even reverse the effects of early-life disadvantage. From this perspective, sharing mindfulness with adolescents holds more promise and importance.

THE CHALLENGES OF ADOLESCENCE

Those of us who serve adolescents are tasked with helping them navigate the perils and promises of this time. When we fully understand the challenges, risks, and key developmental tasks of this phase, we can offer support in more meaningful ways.

Volatility and Risk Taking

Neuroscientists have noted that distinct brain systems mature at different points in development. During the rapid changes of adolescent brain development, the dynamic relationship between brain systems may be unbalanced.

This idea has been formulated in the "dual systems model" (Shulman, 2016), which proposes that adolescent behavior reflects the *early maturation* of the incentive–reward processing system but the *underdevelopment* of the cognitive control system. The incentive–processing system (associated with craving, reward reinforcement, and habit formation) focuses on novel, sensation-seeking, and often risky behaviors. The cognitive control system constrains these impulses toward pleasure and novelty. Scientists suggest that the asynchronous development of these brain systems creates an imbalance that may be responsible for the risky behavior of adolescents. In other words, adolescents have the same impulses for pleasure and novelty as adults, but lack some of the capacities for self-reflection and impulse control.

The most dire consequence of adolescents' impulsivity and risk taking is the high rate of death and disability for this age group. Although the bodily health and strength of adolescents is at a developmental peak, their physical safety is put at risk by their emotional volatility and underdeveloped cognitive control skills. Ronald Dahl (2004), who conducted a global program of adolescent research, powerfully describes this paradox:

> Compared to young children, adolescents are stronger, bigger, and faster, and are achieving maturational improvements in reaction time, reasoning abilities, immune function, and the capacity to withstand cold, heat, injury, and physical stress. In almost every measurable domain, this is *a developmental period of strength and resilience*. Yet, despite these robust maturational improvements in several domains, overall morbidity and mortality rates *increase* 200% over the same interval of time. This doubling in rates of death and disability from the period of early school age into late adolescence and early adulthood is not the result of cancer, heart disease, or mysterious infections. Rather, the major sources of death and disability in adolescence are related to *difficulties in the control of behavior and emotion*. It is the high rates of accidents, suicide, homicide, depression, alcohol and sub-

stance abuse, violence, reckless behaviors, eating disorders, and health problems related to risky sexual behaviors that are killing many youth in our society. (p. 3)

Sensitivity to Social Stress

Another hallmark of this period is that adolescents develop a more nuanced understanding of their own mind and the minds of others. This process is closely related to the effort to form a coherent identity. Adolescents develop a more sophisticated *theory of mind*, which means they are able to attribute to another individual mental states that differ from their own. In other words, they recognize that others have their own distinct moods, feelings, and reactions, and that these may differ considerably from their own internal state. As the theory of mind develops within adolescents, they begin to recognize that they are also an *object* in the minds of others. This realization—that others also see you independently from the way you see yourself—leads to heightened self-consciousness. Social evaluation and sensitivity to group norms is especially prominent in the minds of adolescents, a fact that can be observed not just anecdotally but even detected in the patterns of brain activity. Recently, a British woman posted her diary entry for July 20, 1969, highlighting the particular developmental quality of adolescence: "I went to arts centre (by myself!) in yellow cords and blouse. Ian was there but he didn't speak to me. Got rhyme put in my handbag from someone who's apparently got a crush on me. It's Nicholas I think. UGH. Man landed on moon."

Social evaluation is such a reliable catalyst of stress for humans that research paradigms use the threat of social disapproval to study stress experimentally. As a graduate student, Matthew worked on a study of adolescent development and early life trauma, which included studying stress hormone responses. Adolescents participating in the study would be required to tell a story that would be judged for creativity and then asked to perform math problems in their head and share the answers aloud. The supposed judges (unfamiliar adults wearing white lab coats) would sit, expressionless, with clipboards and rating forms. Researchers collected saliva samples from the adolescent subject to assess stress hormone reactivity. As you might imagine, this situation would reliably provoke a stress response. Such a process is stressful even for adults. For teens, with their acute sensitivity to social evaluation, it was especially intense. (And it was probably the worst part of graduate school for Matthew, who was charged with conducting the test.) The results were consistent with what we know about social anxiety among adolescents: that the development of a stable identity makes social evaluation especially fraught.

Of course, the threat of negative judgment coexists with the promise of positive judgment. We've all seen how social media platforms capitalize on the potency of these psychological forces in adolescents; students compulsively check their feeds, hoping for positive feedback from peers. Technology exploits our human social vulnerabilities, playing off of the fear of exclusion and missing out to foster greater compulsivity. Social media platforms glorify social status and feed potent psychological forces of comparison, envy, vengefulness, and tribalism. Remaining aware of adolescents' acute sensitivity to social evaluation can inform how we teach mindfulness. It encourages us to tend carefully to the group system, to maximize emotional safety, and to be exquisitely sensitive to the operation of social hierarchies and the dynamics of inclusion, ostracism, and peer pressure.

Identity Formation and Autonomy

> **TRY THIS . . .**
> Name three ways you identify yourself from the inside (e.g., shy, creative, feminine). Name three ways the world identities you (e.g., brown-skinned, tall, male). **Reflection question**: Recognize how these may differ. How does this affect your experience of identity?

Out of this cauldron of social-evaluative threat and opportunity, adolescents experience the pressure to forge an identity. Erik Erikson (1968) famously described adolescence as a time of identity formation or role confusion, when adolescents differentiate from their parents or caretakers and work to integrate the various roles they inhabit into a coherent identity. Adolescents are transitioning from being children who like some things and dislike others to being people with certain qualities that they value and are valued for having. They parade these positive qualities for others, while shamefully concealing what they consider to be weaknesses. In some sense, they become a character they are themselves crafting: a person with a past and with qualities that point toward a particular future.

The volatility of the adolescent years reflects the precariousness of this process. The symbolic presence of parents or caretakers looms large as adolescents explore and test new identities. The complexity of dependence, love, ambivalence, resentment, pride, and shame all inform the task of identity development. Adolescents at once emulate their parents while seeking to differentiate from them. In his novel, *Straight Man*, Richard Russo (1997) writes, "The world is divided between kids who grow up wanting to be their parents and those like us, who grow up wanting to be anything but. Neither group ever succeeds" (p. 371). This parental conflict often exhibited during adolescence reflects, in part, the attempt to grapple with the goodness and pain of one's familial experience.

Balancing Authority and Motivation

CONSIDER THIS . . .

One of the greatest personal lessons we can learn when working with adolescents is that we do not have to be their friend. We are there to offer what we can as adults, mentors, and elders. We do not have to show up as anyone other than ourselves or give them more than the best we have to offer.

Not surprisingly, the themes that animate adolescents' relationship with their parents inform their relationship to authority more generally. Adolescent rebellion and suspicion of authority must be carefully harnessed in order to teach mindfulness effectively. How we, as teachers, hold our authority is incredibly important. If we can align with the adolescents in a manner that respects their autonomy while maintaining our role as a leader, the learning can be especially healing. Adolescents benefit deeply from experiencing power that is reasoned, nonarbitrary, and exercised with care and respect.

One of the core principles in this book is that mindfulness teachers need to meet adolescents where they are. We aren't trying to impose our values on them nor are we trying to manufacture aspirations that they lack. Instead, we're capitalizing on the commitments and values they already hold, leveraging their authentic interests and motivations in productive directions. For example, there is a line of research around adolescent diet that has very important lessons for mindfulness teachers.

A Healthy Eating Intervention

In the past 40 years, we have witnessed an increase in obesity that is considered a global epidemic; this is particularly acute in the United States. As the health and economic implications became clear, pediatricians, researchers, school administrators, and public health officials determined that interventions were necessary. But as detailed by Christopher Bryan (Bryan et al., 2016), a behavioral scientist who studies influence and persuasion, the programs designed to create healthier eating among adolescents assumed incorrectly that adolescents would be motivated to be healthier in the distant future. This didn't mean the teens were apathetic, as is often assumed, just that their motivations lay elsewhere. As the authors write:

Adolescents are known to be highly motivated to live up to important values that are shared with their peers, most likely as a means to demonstrate their value to the peer group . . . We propose that it is possible instead to harness this desire as a driver of positive behavior. We seek to do this by aligning the behavior (healthy eating) with important, widely shared adolescent values. Two such values are autonomy and a concern for social justice. (p. 10830)

Rather than focusing on the long-term benefits of healthy eating, the authors designed a healthy eating intervention that was framed in terms of their values. They continue:

[We designed it] as an exposé of manipulative food industry marketing practices designed to influence and deceive adolescents and others into eating larger quantities of unhealthy foods than they otherwise would choose to eat. . . . [W]e cast the executives behind food marketing as controlling adult authority figures and framed the avoidance of junk food as a way to rebel against their control. Second, we emphasized the social justice consequences of these manipulative industry practices: for example, disproportionately targeting poor people and very young children with advertisements for the unhealthiest products. (p. 10831)

The authors found that this angle, compared with an approach based on improving future health, increased the social status of healthy eating and created an alignment between healthy eating and values of autonomy and social justice. Further, adolescents receiving the intervention were more likely to forego sugary snacks and drinks in favor of healthier options. The authors suggest that for adolescents, the immediate symbolic reward of feeling aligned with their own values is a more potent motivator than the distant promise of future health.

Such findings highlight again a key aspect of teaching mindfulness to adolescents: the practice must be relevant to their current concerns rather than attempt to transform those concerns. Honoring the thirst for autonomy and peer acceptance can win the trust and interest of adolescents. (We'll explore this in more depth in Chapter 5). Mindfulness lessons can harness these potent forces to motivate practice and prosocial behavior.

PUTTING DEVELOPMENTAL THEORY INTO PRACTICE

How can these themes directly inform our teaching? Let's step outside the school context for a minute and enter the world of mindfulness retreats in order to illustrate how mindfulness teachings can be tailored to fit the specific developmental needs of adolescents.

Mindfulness retreats provide an intensive experience of silence and stillness. Each of the authors has spent extensive time—cumulatively, years—in silent, intensive mindfulness retreat. Traditionally, retreats for adults are rigorous, demanding affairs. Retreatants wake up early, around 5:00 a.m., and alternately practice sitting and walking meditation until about 10:00 p.m. All of this is done predominantly in silence; participants do not read, write, or speak (except to periodically ask questions of the teachers). Retreatants relinquish media, technology, and all other forms of potential distraction. Their only task is attending to their moment-to-moment experience of being alive: sitting, walking, eating, bathing, resting, and transitioning. Although this may sound like deprivation, retreatants are often surprised to find great insight and kindness emerging through the practice.

In the early 1990s, a group of Insight Meditation teachers, having respect for the retreat form, sought to adapt it so that it might adequately meet the needs of adolescents. They wanted to provide a rich, immersive experience of silence and simplicity, while honoring the developmental stage of adolescents. For the teens, the silent retreat format morphed into something of a combination of a retreat, summer camp, and group support. Based on their experiments, the current schedule for most teen mindfulness retreats combines periods of silent practice with small group work, workshops, free time, and a community performance and celebration. The kids enter and exit periods of silent mindfulness practice (sitting and walking) guided by the teachers. They practice in silence for between 4 and 5 hours each day, while having generous amounts of downtime and periods of connection.

While you may not be planning to offer residential retreats for teenagers, there's much to be learned from how these retreats have evolved over many years. During that process, key points emerged about creating mindfulness programs that are relevant for teens in any context.

Consider carefully the age of participants. Initially, retreats included teens aged 13 years and older. Experience demonstrated that a 15-year-old minimum age requirement was more effective. After each retreat, the leaders would carefully evaluate the components of the retreat that served the teens and those aspects that needed change or augmentation. Key aspects of the retreat were shaped to suit the self-regulatory and social needs of adolescents. Although data are insufficient to make firm conclusions, there is some preliminary evidence that older adolescents benefit more from intensive mindfulness programming than do middle schoolers.

Find the optimal dose of silent practice. Adolescents need robust connections with peers to balance the solitude of time spent in silence. Thus, the teen retreat was modified to include several daily periods of connection. A 2- or 3-hour silent period of practice in the morning is followed by hours of peer connection. In classrooms, intersperse silent practice with periods of interaction and peer connection.

Facilitate regular, meaningful connection between students. A primary vehicle for connection in intensive teen retreats is the small group format. Teens are assigned, according to age, to groups of approximately eight. Twice a day, following periods of silence, teens meet in these small groups for 1 hour to explore and digest with peers their experiences of silence. Structure the discussion with clear guidelines for interaction and suggested prompts.

Decide on a system for adult facilitation. In retreats, each group is co-facilitated by two adult staff whose primary role is to set the *container*, a social climate characterized by trust, emotional safety, and authenticity. Creating a strong container allows healthy connections to unfold. Adults are typically most effective when they are least prominent in the group.

Step back and highlight the adolescents. On adult retreats, participants commonly celebrate the teachers, expressing gratitude and praise. On teen retreats, the adolescents celebrate *each other* and the emotional freedom engendered by the community. Teachers provide structure and the assurance of emotional safety, then step back and allow adolescents to explore their own connections. Their interactions are often deeply poignant, featuring high levels of emotional disclosure as they share difficult experiences, celebrate insights, and bear witness to the heart-opening transformations that commonly unfold in the silence.

Balance supervision with choice and autonomy. Honoring the autonomy of the adolescents begins before they even arrive at the retreat. Teens are screened to ensure that they, rather than parents or caretakers, are genuinely motivated to participate. Ambivalent feelings are fine, but there must be a kernel of intrinsic interest; otherwise the retreat is unlikely to be a positive experience. (Mandatory mindfulness programming will probably alienate a significant proportion of any group.) Providing some basis for self-selection and honoring the individual's autonomy are important conditions for mindfulness practice.

Co-create agreements on conduct. The teachers craft agreements with the adolescents in a way that isn't perceived as an arbitrary imposition of power. Teachers explain the rationale for the agreements: rather than a moralistic or puritan agenda, they aim to foster an atmosphere of respect and nonharming. The journey of a mindfulness retreat (or course) cannot be undertaken without a backdrop of care. Safety is the precondition for self-exploration and self-acceptance. On retreats, this includes a commitment to abstain from drugs, alcohol, and sexual behavior for the duration of the program. Often, one or two teens who have previously attended a retreat will come to the front of the room and offer a few words on the rationale for these ethical commitments.

They are often sincere, articulate, and persuasive in appealing for a commitment from the entire group.

Invite rather than demand participation. How we introduce mindfulness practice on a teen retreat differs substantially in tone from adult retreats. Adolescents are highly sensitive to the arbitrary imposition of authority. We begin with the authentic concerns of the teens and then introduce how mindfulness might be relevant for navigating this realm. Leaders must demonstrate their genuine concern for the well-being of the adolescents. This silent transmission of care makes the imposition of authority acceptable. When the intention of the leader is wholesome, a different kind of relationship is possible with the teens.

Skilled teaching and true empathic connection entail fully honoring the inner lives of adolescents. As we will see throughout this book, these particular developmental themes of adolescence inform every aspect of our teaching: from program design to setting, from lesson structure to specific interventions. When we understand and care for our students' state of mind, they will tend to extend a measure of goodwill. It is through this doorway that we walk to share the practice of mindfulness.

CHAPTER 3

You Are the Instrument: Personal Practice and Embodied Teaching

Each day at the beginning of class Mr. Levin stood at the front of the room, hands clasped in front of his chest just above his slightly rounded belly, and took a slow, deep breath. He looked out across the room with a steady gaze and smile. Once we had quietly arrived together, the day's lesson in high school physics would begin. We all learned a lot in his class that year, but the most important thing was a different kind of physics—a sort of interpersonal alchemy whereby the gravity of his presence calmed and soothed our own. I never forgot those moments of Mr. Levin silently greeting the class with a full heart, nor the seamless combination of kindness, patience, and enthusiasm with which he taught. Without realizing it, my awkward teenage body relaxed in this teacher's presence.

MAYA ANGELOU FAMOUSLY QUIPPED, "I'VE LEARNED that people will forget what you said, people will forget what you did, but people will never forget how you made them feel." We invite you to pause and consider: Who were the teachers or mentors who had the greatest positive impact in your life? Who inspired you? What was it about them that left that mark? We're willing to bet it was less what they taught and more how you felt in their presence.

As we explored in Chapter 1, mindfulness practice is the cultivation of a clear and balanced awareness. It's about learning to live life from a baseline of nonreactive awareness, rather than accumulating information or esoteric knowledge about contemplative practice. The question is, what impact does the development of direct, openhearted awareness have on one's teaching and facilitation skills? What we've seen in countless educators is that the embodiment of mindfulness confers benefits on *both* teachers and students. The cultivation of awareness not only provides an essential foundation for sharing mindfulness-based interventions, but is an invaluable asset for teaching in general, no matter the topic or student population.

Teaching mindfulness depends on our own understanding of the practice, as well as on our ability to embody that practice in the flow of our teaching. The personal practice of mindfulness supports a well-regulated, wholehearted presence. That presence allows a teacher to develop relationships of genuine connection with students. An authentic relationship, in turn, forms the foundation of effective curriculum delivery.

FINDING OUR WAY

Educators come to the work of teaching young people and adolescents through many different doors. You may have known a mentor who had a particularly strong impact on you during your own adolescence and long to serve and give back in a similar way. Or, conversely, you may have *lacked* key input from adults at that crucial juncture in your life and struggled to find your way; many adolescents contend with overwhelming emotions, doubt, depression, or addiction. You may feel a strong affinity for that age in life and take great pleasure in connecting during this formative period of development.

However we end up in the room, teaching is hard work. There is often a range of structural challenges: inadequate funding, large class sizes, lack of administrative support or leadership, high stress, and, in some circumstances, even a measure of social isolation. In addition, we bump up against the complexity of the young human beings who sit before us, as well as the limitations of our own capacity for patience, empathy, or compassion.

With the obstacles of today's education system, as well as the unique challenges of teaching adolescents, it's easy to lose sight of the one of the most important parts of teaching—our relationships with the kids. A significant amount of learning occurs through relationships. Mindfulness can be understood as the bedrock of healthy relationship-building. Before we say anything, it is our ability *to be here* in a relaxed and balanced way that creates the conditions for connection, learning, and meaningful exchange.

Sometimes, teaching mindfulness with adolescents is relegated to a lower status compared with training adults. Accordingly, the standards for trainers are typically lower. We believe this is a mistake—adolescents deserve and can distinctly benefit from trainers with the highest level of expertise. In fact, having a personal mindfulness practice and embodying it while teaching are the foundations of effective mindfulness-based interventions.

Yet educators today take a weekend workshop in mindfulness, or pick up a book, and believe that this is enough to begin sharing the practice. The skills of teaching mindfulness go beyond the ordinary requirements for subject-matter competence. Mindfulness practice is different from purely academic subjects in that it's not simply about transmitting information. The development of a teacher's own mindful awareness has a direct impact on their ability to facilitate others' learning of the practice. It's like trying to teach someone to swim when you've never been in the water. You need direct experience with mindfulness to teach it—and your embodied expression of mindfulness transmits a confidence in the path of practice.

Effectively sharing mindfulness with teenagers is a unique competence that depends on distinct skill sets. It requires developing facility in a range of overlapping areas: an understanding of mindfulness meditation; proficiency in teaching and explaining subtle concepts in clear and accessible ways; and a flexible, relaxed, and authentic capacity to connect with adolescents.

When done well, teaching mindfulness to teens can be incredibly joyful.

The teacher capitalizes on salient developmental characteristics of teens—identity formation, heightened awareness of meaning, sensitivity to group norms, skepticism regarding authority—in order to more effectively transmit the practice. By establishing the relevance of mindfulness for key developmental challenges, and by highlighting innate strengths and qualities in teens, the teacher can connect with adolescents in an authentic and deeply meaningful way.

Meditation teachers Megan Cowan and Chris McKenna, cofounder and former Program Director of Mindful Schools (respectively), suggest that we understand the process of teaching mindfulness as having three parts, each of which builds on and informs the development of the other two. The model is circular, with the relationship between the components building over time.

1. **Personal Practice:** The foundation of teaching mindfulness is one's own development and continuing cultivation of both formal and informal mindfulness practice, which helps us to attune more keenly to our own internal experience. Mindfulness practice serves as a field guide to the heart and mind. We cannot understand the joys and sorrows, the fears and longing of others, unless we have had an intimate encounter with our own heart. Without this as a foundation, *Embodied Teaching* cannot be accessed.

2. **Embodied Teaching:** The second foundation of teaching mindfulness is embodying mindful awareness and its associated positive qualities in one's teaching (e.g., patience, kindness, empathy, generosity). We train not only to *teach mindfulness*, but to become *mindful teachers*. As educators, we are not merely dispensing information; we also are embodying and modeling mindfulness itself. In this sense, you are the medium and "the medium is the message," to quote media critic Marshall McLuhan. During this phase, one transfers and refines the learning from personal practice into the space of relationship as well as into group facilitation skills. Without embodied teaching, *Curriculum Delivery* often has mixed results.

3. **Curriculum Delivery:** The first two foundations directly inform and enhance our ability to implement mindfulness-based curricula with varied adolescent populations in educational, institutional, and therapeutic contexts. The ability to deliver lessons, customize content, and share in an authentic and relevant way depends upon our understanding and embodiment of the practice.

YOUR NERVOUS SYSTEM IS THE INTERVENTION

These three foundations of mindfulness-based interventions can be understood from another, more general pedagogical perspective. We can consider teaching along three primary axes: there is *what* you teach, the content and subject matter you are sharing (curriculum delivery); there is *how* you teach, your manner, internal state, and interpersonal and relational skills (embodied teaching); and there is *who* you teach, the identity of your students, complete with their personal, emotional, and social histories. Personal practice informs both *how* you teach, as well as your ability to attune to and connect with *who* you teach.

Traditional public education has focused primarily on what we teach, on pedagogy and the transfer of knowledge in which the student is an empty vessel to be filled. In the United States at present, the content to be learned is codified by the Common Core State Standards (and the state standards largely based on them) and assessed at increasingly frequent intervals with standardized tests. More humanistic and child-centered approaches place a greater emphasis on *how* we teach, recognizing that the method of delivery can be as (if not more) important than the content, and according less importance to external evaluation of what is learned. Here, attention is given not only to different strengths but to the educator's expression of social and emotional intelligence as a key factor in student learning.

However, from the perspective of interpersonal neurobiology (an interdisciplinary approach to understanding human development and functioning through the interaction of social and biological realms), the internal state of the educator plays an underlying role in creating the classroom culture, emotional environment, and learning experience of students. This perspective—that our internal state, level of awareness, and self-regulation matter, especially with children and adolescents—runs counter to conventional assumptions and mainstream educational theory. Yet today we are learning more and more about how intricately our nervous systems affect one another and how important the presence of healthy, well-regulated adults is for the development of basic skills like self-regulation, self-soothing, and impulse control, as well as the maturity of neurological structures and functions that support these skills.

A parallel in psychotherapy research helps to illustrate this point. On the one hand, there are different therapeutic techniques with different theoretical orientations. Depression might be treated with cognitive behavioral therapy or interpersonal therapy. Some scientists have suggested we have focused excessively on differences in technique and not enough on the characteristics of the therapist. In fact, findings consistently document that the therapist and their capacity to form a good therapeutic alliance exert powerful effects on the success or failure of the treatment. In much the same way, students will benefit from educators developing mindfulness and relational skills.

Humans are not born with completely developed brains and nervous systems. As infants, the capacity for self-regulation is absent. Infants' nervous systems are immature and not yet independently capable of managing intense stimuli. The caregiver acts as the soothing system until the infant's nervous system is developed and can begin to regulate itself. This is one of the reasons why contact, mirroring, and empathy are so essential in the first months and years of life. The bodily warmth and steady heartbeat of physical contact, eye contact and facial expressions, and words and tone of voice all help to soothe and regulate the developing nervous systems of infants.

As children mature past infancy, adults and caregivers still play a role in the regulation of their nervous systems. Even in adolescence, brain function is different from that of mature adulthood (about 25 years of age). Cortical regions of the brain continue to mature into the 20s. As we've explored previously, the neurobiology of adolescents predisposes them to higher levels of impulsivity and challenges with longer term planning. Clinical social worker Arlene Montgomery (2013), of the University of Texas–Austin, highlights the importance of kind others in developing self-regulation:

> Human beings are dependent on mature brains to initially assist in the microregulation of their physical and emotional world. Ideally, this interactive regulation transitions back and forth over the childhood and adolescence until the person is largely self-regulating. However, at stressful times, it is necessary and appropriate to seek interactive regulation from stable others. (p. 197)

Our students' bodies and brains are responding to the state of our own nervous system. As teachers, if we are present, stable, and available, we can play a pivotal role in helping young people to self-regulate.

The issue then becomes, what's the condition of our nervous system when we are interacting with young people? How much do we prioritize attunement? Are we prioritizing awareness and responsiveness in our teaching and interactions with young people? Is the quality of our attention and presence at least as important as the explicit content we are delivering in class? Are we present, internally balanced, and empathic? Or are we burned out, fatigued, anxious, or perpetually distressed in our classrooms, schools, and therapy offices? If so, we are on some level transmitting this to the young people we teach and failing to provide the essential support their immature nervous systems need to grow and develop properly.

Our experience doing this work with thousands of young people suggests that *cultivating mindful awareness while teaching is an intervention in its own right, even if we never teach mindfulness explicitly to our students.* Thus, the role of personal practice includes the development of our own resilience—in service of our own well-being as well in the service of the support and well-being of our students.

As author and educator Parker Palmer (2007) notes, "We teach who we are" (p. 1). Mr. Levin, Oren's high school physics teacher, said more about how much he cared in those few moments at the beginning of each class than some teachers say in an entire year. Again, think back to your own experiences with teachers who inspired you or made a lasting, positive mark on your life. More than what they said or did, perhaps even more than how they treated you, there is something intangible yet felt in the presence of another human being who is genuinely present, kind, and compassionate.

In his book, *You Are Special: Words of Wisdom for All Ages from a Beloved Neighbor,* the educator, minister, and TV personality Fred Rogers (1995) wrote, "Everyone longs to be loved. And the greatest thing we can do is to let people know that they are loved and capable of loving" (p. 10). Mindfulness gives us a tool, a concrete practice to begin to realize the possibility of helping adolescents to experience their own lovability.

NONVERBAL INFORMATION

Let's dig a little deeper into what's going on in the classroom between educators and students. As human beings we are by nature deeply social and empathic creatures who experience the world through our senses. We feel and are affected by our environment and by our fellow human beings. Beginning to understand and live in alignment with this fundamental sensitivity is key to practicing and teaching mindfulness.

In his work with Mindful Schools, Chris McKenna describes how mindfulness practice gives us access to a greater amount of kinesthetic information. He notes that many of us living in modern societies exist with a kind of "feeling-deficit," and that it can take some people time to recover the ability to feel even gross physical sensations (Mindful Schools, 2018). Mindfulness of the body opens up entire areas of sensation and information that were previously unconscious and helps us to develop an awareness of what philosopher and therapist Eugene Gendlin (1981) called "the felt sense." The felt sense can be understood as somatic awareness of our overall experience in any given moment. Gendlin defined it as a "special kind of internal bodily awareness . . . a body-sense of meaning" (p. 10).

McKenna goes on to state that alongside the factual and conceptual information we teach, a large body of nonverbal information passes back and forth between the educator and students. Our posture, gaze, and the angle of our head can communicate self-assured confidence and well-being, or uncertainty and heavy-heartedness. The pace, tone, and rhythm of our voice may send a message of ease and relaxation ("there's plenty of time to learn this material"); one of consternation and stress ("we don't really have time for this"); or of boredom and disconnection ("why am I here in this room going over this pointless material?").

Similarly, the body language, tone of voice, facial expressions, and behaviors of our students transmit a world of information about their state of being, emotions, and level of interest. A skilled educator is able to intuitively track much of this in the room overall as well as in individual students and to adjust their own presence and nonverbal communication to reassure, calm, soothe, encourage, or steady their students' inner state as needed.

In the last few decades, we've begun to understand more about the way humans transmit information nonverbally. Psychologist and emotion researcher Paul Ekman has done significant work on what are known as *microexpressions*, momentary facial expressions of emotion that involuntarily flash across our visage when we are attempting to hide a feeling. In these moments, we involuntarily reveal our true feelings in spite of conscious attempts to conceal them. Microexpressions often register just below the surface of consciousness in those observing them, such that we may have a felt sense of another's emotional state without being able to say exactly why.

Another phenomenon that points to a deeper connection between our internal states is known as *emotional contagion*—which is exactly what it sounds like. We pick up on and begin to feel the emotions of others around us. Humans often unconsciously mimic the facial expressions, vocal expressions, bodily postures, and physical behaviors of those around us. In doing so, we end up *catching* their emotions. We can observe this manifestation of mirroring in the most ordinary of moments. Ever notice how easy it is to pick up on someone else's anxiety and start to feel a bit on edge yourself? Or the inverse, how joy and laughter can be infectious? Emotional contagion has even been observed among newborns in the hospital. If one baby begins crying, others nearby are likely to begin expressing distress and crying.

In the 1990s, neuroscientists made a groundbreaking discovery into the presence of what are known as *mirror neurons*, a small circuit of specialized cells in the premotor cortex and inferior parietal cortex that fire both when we ourselves perform an action (e.g., smiling, or lifting a glass) and when we observe someone else performing an action. These neurons collapse the distinction between doing and seeing. When I observe someone else perform a certain action or movement, part of my brain engages, mirroring the movement as if I were doing it myself. The mirror neuron system is a direct motor component of empathy, which neuroscientists have linked to the development of cognitive empathy (Haker, Kawohl, Herwig & Rössler, 2013). In other words, if I perceive an angry expression on your face, my brain registers the neural signature of anger, which leads to an intuitive understanding of your felt experience.

Marco Iacoboni, a neuroscientist at UCLA's Ahmanson-Lovelace Brain Mapping Center, writes:

> What do we do when we interact? We use our body to communicate our intentions and our feelings. The gestures, facial expressions, body postures we make are social signals, ways of communicating with one another. The way mirror neurons likely let us understand others is by

providing some kind of inner imitation of the actions of other people, which in turn leads us to "simulate" the intentions and emotions associated with those actions. When I see you smiling, my mirror neurons for smiling fire up, too, initiating a cascade of neural activity that evokes the feeling we typically associate with a smile. I don't need to make any inference on what you are feeling, I experience immediately and effortlessly (in a milder form, of course) what you are experiencing. (Iacoboni & Lerner, 2008, p. 21)

Ever notice how kids seem to be able to read exactly what's happening for you? Or how immediately adolescents detect a lack of authenticity in adults? Think of all the times you just had a hunch something might be going on for one of your students and asked, only to find you were spot on?

Who and how you are registers with students nonverbally and is continually confirmed or adjusted as we engage. If we're on edge, stressed, or experiencing some inner conflict about being in the room, students sense this. It will register with particular significance for young people with trauma who are hypervigilant and continually assessing their environment for threat or safety. *Absent* adults are too common in the lives of young people—an especially big problem for those at high risk. If you're not fully present, or if your internal state isn't congruent with your verbal expression, you may become inadvertently associated with all of the other adults in a child's life who are not present or reliable. In these moments, it's that much harder for young people to trust you and relax in your presence.

Using One's Presence to Shape the Emotional Atmosphere

You can experiment with this flow of nonverbal information by paying attention to the felt sense in your own body, noticing subtle changes, feelings, or intuition in relation to your students or the room as a whole. McKenna suggests one primary way to support the process of coregulation is to focus your awareness on your own sense of grounded embodiment and tune in to any sense of solidity. You may experience this as a sense that you are simultaneously grounded and stable while also feeling empty or transparent. One feels soft and open but unshakable.

As personal practice matures, this sense of being grounded becomes the new set point for our nervous system and can be an important asset in teaching. It's easier to be fully present in your own body and take up space in the room. This can be particularly helpful if the level of dysregulation in the class is high. Your grounded presence serves as a kind of surrogate for the class, allowing the students to anchor onto your stabilized and well-regulated system. Standing mindfully is an excellent practice for developing this skill. Stand comfortably, spine erect, in a stable, upright posture. Bend your knees slightly and sink the attention into your body, sensing its alignment and relaxing your muscles and tissues.

Another practice based on the flow of nonverbal information that can enhance coregulation is consciously modulating the prosody of your voice: its volume, pitch, tone, pace, and rhythm. The quality of the voice is one of the primary ways humans and other large-brained mammals attune to and regulate each other. While teaching, explore the effect on your own level of awareness as well as the quality of attention in the room as you bring more mindfulness to the process of speaking. Try ending some sentences on a higher tone and others on a low tone. Increase your pace, then slow it down and pause for effect. Explore how such shifts in your voice change your ability to be more mindful, present, and grounded.

BEING REAL WITH KIDS:
INNER AND OUTER CONGRUENCE

As humans, we are continually making meaning. We long to live in a coherent world where our own choices and the actions of those around us make sense. When our internal state and behavior don't match, others are left to fill in the gap and make sense of the discrepancy. The stories that we create to explain others' behavior often have more to do with our previous life experiences, expectations, and core beliefs than the actual data in front of us.

One white educator, we'll call him "John,"* recounted the following experience. He was visiting a high school in the inner city to teach mindfulness for the first time. Having grown up in a predominantly white suburb, he was unfamiliar with the environment of an urban high school, with mostly African American and Latino students. John had attended several diversity and anti-oppression workshops, and felt committed to being more aware of how his own unconscious racism might impact his ability to serve students most effectively.

During the first class, he felt tense. He wanted so much for things to go right—to connect with the teens and inspire them to want to learn about mindfulness. In response, he was pretty nervous. The awkwardness showed in his posture, his tone, and the pacing of his speech. As he began talking about why he was here and what he hoped to share with them, the students began shifting in their seats and making comments under their breath. He could tell something was off; they definitely weren't connecting.

John paused and took a deep breath. He decided to take a risk and spoke to what was happening. "It seems like you all aren't quite vibing with me yet. Anyone want to tell me what's up?" One of the young men spoke up sharply, "You're just like the rest of those white folks; y'all can't stand to be around us." In that moment, John realized what was happening. His state of anxiety was crystal clear to the teens. Without any context for why he felt nervous, they made the most logical conclusion: you're uncomfortable because you're racist and don't like being around folks of color. He spoke to what was happening to see if he could course correct: "Well, you're right about one thing, I'm really

*The name and identifying details of this story have been changed to preserve the privacy of the educator.

nervous. But it's not because I don't like you or don't want to be here. And I can see that trying to pretend I'm not feeling tense isn't helping. I'm nervous because I really care about this stuff that I'm about to share with you, and believe that it can make a huge difference in each of your lives. It's so important to me that I want to do my best to convey it and I'm afraid I won't be able to, and that you'll miss an opportunity to learn something really valuable because of my own shortcomings."

The student responded, "Well, man, why didn't you just say that?" Several of the students in the room started laughing and the energy started to shift. John relaxed and so did the students. They were finally getting off to the right start.

Nonverbal interpersonal communication is a two-way street. As you teach, the teens and adolescents are simultaneously sending you a world of information. John picked up quickly on the verbal and nonverbal signals—eyes looking askance, feet shuffling, the perceivable tension in the air. These were all fairly obvious. With the sharpened faculties and heightened awareness of mindfulness practice, you're able to pick up on even more subtle signals in individuals as well as in the field within the room and to use them to inform your choices in the relationship moment to moment.

Your ability to sense what's happening in the room is directly proportional to your ability to access your own internal state, the felt sense of your own experience. With mindfulness practice, you notice more in the environment and get immediate feedback from your own body about what's happening within you in response. In this way, you can develop the ability to more quickly assess the mood, tone, and energy in the room. In other words, what we might commonly refer to as *intuition* is a learnable skill.

CONSIDER THIS . . .

It's a great practice for adults to reflect on what the day in the life of our students might look like and the particularities of their challenges. Have they been fighting with their best friend, are their parents getting divorced, have they moved into a new neighborhood, are they dealing with a pet that died, going home to an empty house every day, or dealing with other stressors?

Over time, your ability to respond appropriately to the unique circumstances of each moment increases. Instead of needing to cognitively strategize how to address a situation, a response can arise from your own wisdom, experience, and the needs of the moment. In John's situation, he trusted his gut instinct and chose to disclose transparently what was happening for him. This undercut the dynamic of mistrust that was based on the incongruity between his inner state and his actions. In meeting the situation directly, his response simultaneously defused the tension, built trust, and started to create the conditions for a more authentic conversation.

MATURING THROUGH AWARENESS

Mindfulness practice involves a radical investigation of what it is to be human. Through the steady application of attention in formal practice, you discern changes in physical sensations and emotions, as well as habitual thought patterns and their relationship to emotions. As you look more deeply, you will become more familiar with the underlying causes of the distress and emotional pain in life. You can see how past wounds inform and shape our experience of the present and how our preferences and biases are rooted in certain beliefs, assumptions, or old hurts. Over time, this enhances your ability to more effectively handle stress reactivity and strong emotions.

This awareness carries over into daily activities. You can expand your ability to notice the flow of changing emotions and sensations during the day and develop the capacity to feel and manage your affective state with more balance. For example, during heavy traffic on your commute, if you notice tension and frustration in your body, mindfulness supports you to attend to the reactivity in the moment rather than allowing it to build. With practice, you can learn to leave the stress of the commute in the past rather than carrying it with you into every interaction of the day.

These skills transfer directly to our teaching. If we have an argument with a student, mindfulness allows us to let go and move on so that we see that student with fresh eyes the next day instead of carrying a perception about the student from the past and relating to the student through that filter.

With mindfulness, habitual behaviors and reactivity become a signal for deeper investigation. Instead of getting caught in the emotions or their underlying stories, instead of blaming external conditions (e.g., a student, colleague, or administrator), you can turn the attention inward to discern where you are getting *hooked*. You recognize that the student who knows just how to push your buttons reminds you of a sibling or yourself at a younger age. It dawns on you that the intense frustration, helplessness, or anger you feel toward the kid who keeps acting out is remarkably akin to how you felt at an earlier time in your life. You begin to be able to distinguish between the observable data of the present and the stories and interpretations we tell and then mistake for reality. Rather than life feeling like a maze to solve, you can approach experience itself as a teacher, highlighting ways to let go, develop wisdom, and mature the heart.

Through this process, mindfulness practice shines the light of awareness on all corners of our minds, revealing our biases in teaching. We become more aware of which students we are likely to favor and with which ones we're more likely to have a shorter fuse. We may see how our social or class conditioning, heteronormative expectations, gender relations, or unconscious racism may show up in our teaching or relationships with students. If unaware of these biases, they operate below the threshold of consciousness informing our actions and choices.

As the functioning of the heart and mind become clearer, healing, resolution, and a different kind of freedom become a reality. We begin to have more choice and agency in the ways we relate with students and more flexibility and agency in our teaching.

HANDLING BURNOUT

Working with young people is hard. It's demanding work, and if you're doing it well, you hear the real stories, what kids are feeling on the inside and what they're living with every day: anxiety, depression, abuse, addiction, sexual violence, mental illness, poverty. The heart breaks in the face of the reality of suffering.

Given the intensity of suffering as well as the systemic challenges in work environments, burnout is common in the fields of education, mental health, and youth work in general. The structures of public education, institutions, nonprofit agencies, and clinical treatment facilities often run counter to the well-being of staff and the young people they serve. Many of these structures are characterized by lack of funding, bureaucratic red tape, vicarious trauma, or toxic work environments.

Burnout is a maladaptive response to accumulated or extreme stress characterized by physical or emotional exhaustion, cynicism or numbing out, and diminished meaning or engagement in one's work. It's a depleted, hopeless state that comes from sustained, repeated pressures. The signs and symptoms of burnout include:

+ Irritability or feeling numbed out
+ Sleep disturbance
+ Difficulty concentrating, absenteeism
+ Substance abuse, depression, feelings of isolation
+ Empathetic dysregulation (either over engaging with or avoiding others' pain)
+ Poor boundaries between work and home life
+ Diminished sense of quality of life

Sometimes, the prescription of mindfulness or other self-care practices serves to deflect the need for more systemic change. As we've mentioned, mindfulness is not a replacement for the creation of structural changes that support teacher well-being. We have significant work to do to address the structural factors that create stress and lead to burnout in educational environments. Alongside this work, mindfulness does provide a powerful tool for resilience, helping us to manage stress levels in the service of being more present and available for teens and adolescents.

Compassion fatigue is an often related but distinct phenomenon that may occur together with burnout or on its own. Compassion fatigue can manifest as a state of tension and preoccupation with the suffering of others, or the opposite, a state of numbness and indifference. It comes from repeated exposure to others' pain or trauma when there is an overidentification of one's own role in the healing or resolution of that pain. It's getting caught in a mental loop about the kid who has suffered terribly and you can't stop thinking about it . . . or the reverse, when you feel nothing in response to such a situation.

Resilience is one's ability to respond to stress in an adaptive way. It's our capacity to bounce back from difficulty and move with ease through cycles of stress and resolution. Neuroscientist, author, and meditation researcher Richard Davidson (2012) defines resilience as "the rapidity with which one recovers from adversity."

In working with teens, having tools to handle burnout and compassion fatigue are essential. Mindfulness practice itself is protective, for all of the reasons mentioned above. It enhances our skills for emotion regulation and stress management, which in turn can support more sustainable energy and increased resilience.

Self-Care

Making self-care a priority is another key tool to protect against burnout. Jessica Morey, mindfulness teacher and executive director of the teen retreat program Inward Bound Mindfulness Education (iBme), points out that martyrdom can be very compelling in this field. "You can burn yourself out with giving and caring. It's important to look honestly at the question, are you taking care of yourself? Are you practicing [mindfulness] on a daily basis?" (personal communication). Many of us may need to actually block out time for exercise, recreation, or meditation in our schedule to make it a priority. When speaking about self-care to her retreat staff, Morey offers a pithy contemplation: Are you treating yourself in ways that you would want the teens to treat themselves? Are you modeling what you're teaching?

CONSIDER THIS . . .

Make it a practice to take on whatever it is that you are asking the kids to do. If you give them a mindfulness assignment, do it yourself. If you are asking them to report back to the class, make sure you do too. This helps both the teacher and the student feel connected in their successes and challenges in the mindfulness practice.

Self-care can mean a lot of different things. Psychologist and author Rick Hanson points to three core human needs that support resilience and protect against burnout: safety, satisfaction, and meaning (2018). Self-care means finding ways to meet these core needs in your life. Regardless of the circumstances of one's work environment, where do you feel safe physically and emotionally? Are you spending time with those people or in those environments, and are you really able to take it in when you're there?

Satisfaction is about the experience of nonaddictive, healthy pleasure when our needs are met. This could be anything from the need to contribute in our work to more personal things like our needs for relaxation, play, enjoyment, connection, and so forth. In your work, do you take the time to notice and really appreciate the small successes? When a student finally *gets* a new concept you're teaching, or comes to class enthusiastically reporting that they used mindfulness to make a different choice in a tense situation, do you allow yourself to pause and relish the moment? In your personal life, step back and consider if you are meeting your own needs for nourishment and rejuvenation. You can't pour from an empty cup. The more we nourish ourselves, the more we have to give.

While youth work can be rich in meaning, it's also common to lose a sense of hope or purpose when faced with the immensity of the task before us. Considering the history of oppression, poverty, institutional racism, or intergenerational trauma, it's easy to begin to feel helpless or overwhelmed, to feel as if nothing we do matters or will make a difference. How do we stay connected to meaning in the face of horror like child abuse, neglect, or disease?

Making space for mourning is an essential part of resilience. As youth educator Morris Ervin quips, "You gotta feel it to heal it" (personal communication). Mindfulness practice is a key resource, offering tools to feel the intensity of our pain and sadness without becoming overwhelmed by it. It's also important to focus on the changes that we *can* make, the good that we can do in our work. While we may not resolve the root causes of poverty, violence, or oppression in our lifetime, we can take joy in knowing that we've helped another human being heal and given that person some inner tools to live a more meaningful life.

Enrique Collazo teaches mindfulness to young people in different contexts and travels the country leading an anti-bullying and violence-prevention program called Challenge Day that breaks down barriers between social cliques and challenges students to create the kind of school community they want. Enrique shared his own process around finding balance with the fine line between caring and compassion fatigue:

> When I first started leading Challenge Days it was really hard to come in and out of a school. I cared so much, I just wanted to take them home. Then I went to the other extreme of really checking out and not being in my body. It took time for me to find the balance and recognize the need for self-care. A big part of my resilience now comes from compassion practice. I go in to the room fully prepared to hold space,

to cry with them, to hold them. After it's done, I let it go. That's the continual practice for me, learning to love and let go. Doing my best to trust deeply in life (personal communication).

Building a Network

Community is another essential resource for protecting against burnout. For many educators running mindfulness programs, the absence of institutional support coupled with the lack of like-minded peers can be a huge obstacle to finding the energy to continue teaching mindfulness. Having a network of like-minded colleagues with whom to celebrate, share ideas, learn, or mourn can balance such challenges. Peers can offer much needed support and assuage the loneliness of working in an institution where there may be few or no colleagues who share your views or goals. Attending conferences or workshops where you can connect with others or joining online programs that have a focus on building community can help you to create such a personal network.

Finally, it's important to remember that burnout is not personal. It is often largely due to systemic factors that are beyond our control. Even with a strong personal practice, self-care routines, and community, you may find that your work situation is simply unsustainable. Many times, educators facing burnout come to the realization that they're simply not willing or able to keep doing what they're doing. The conditions of your workplace may be unacceptable in some way, or you may lack confidence that things are going to change. In these circumstances, you may find that leaving the situation or changing jobs is the only viable solution. We can't help anyone if we ourselves are drowning.

ESTABLISHING A MINDFULNESS PRACTICE

To summarize, having a personal practice is an essential prerequisite for teaching mindfulness:

- It confers intimate understanding of the practice, which is primarily based on direct experience rather than information.
- It refines self-awareness so we can more effectively monitor and handle our own stress and reactivity.
- It creates the conditions for more self-regulation and embodied awareness in the classroom, which begins to affect the nervous systems of the young people and is therefore an intervention in and of itself.
- It enhances our capacity for tracking the flow and exchange of nonverbal information by sharpening cognitive, perceptual, and intuitive awareness.
- It supports resilience and healing, essential factors for working with young people and the institutional cultures.

There are many wonderful resources and options for establishing a personal mindfulness practice—from books and magazines to online courses, podcasts, and apps; from local meditation groups to silent retreats. Books, magazine articles, and audio lectures are all great, but the most important aspect is your own direct experience with the practice. If you're new to the field, here are a few basic pointers to help you get started:

- Begin a daily practice. Aim for 20 minutes or more at roughly the same time each day.
- Consistency, quality of attention, and sincerity of heart are more important than quantity of time. Practicing wholeheartedly for 5 minutes each day is better than skipping all week and trying to catch up by practicing for an hour on Saturday.
- Find community. Whether it's online or in person, connecting with others who are practicing can be incredibly supportive.
- Seek out a teacher or mentor. While technology has increased access to the instruction in dramatic ways, mindfulness practice is best learned in real time from another human being.

- If you can, attend a daylong, weekend, or longer silent retreat. These periods of more intensive practice help advance your understanding and deepen your embodiment of the practice.
- Read and study as you feel inspired. There are countless great books available today. We encourage you to explore the different facets of the practice that interest you.

CHAPTER 4

MUTUAL RESPECT: CREATING CONNECTION AND BUILDING RELATIONSHIP

Jozen asked the teenager: "How are you feeling right now?" "I feel good. But I don't really want to be here. I don't know why I'm here," Jaylin replied. "Why do you think your mom called and reached out?" "I'm going through some anger issues at school—got suspended. But I don't see how this meditation stuff will help me." Jozen remembered appreciating the young man's honesty, his willingness to share so directly and vulnerably. They kept chatting, having an open conversation about what had been going on and how he'd been feeling. They talked about how anger could be useful, that it points to something really important for us, but how it can take over when you get caught up in the emotion. By the end of the conversation an hour later, Jaylin was asking when he could come back. "This is the first time in a long time I've been able to express myself and be heard." Jozen took a deep breath and nodded. "That's real, man" (personal communication).

THE ABOVE DIALOGUE TOOK PLACE AFTER JOZEN Tamori Gibson, in his capacity as youth program director at Brooklyn Zen Center (BZC), received an email from a woman sharing that her son, Jaylin, had been having challenges with anger at school, and asking if Jozen would meet him to see if he could help.

After meeting with Jozen, Jaylin started going to BZC regularly, later joining their 12-week internship program. He graduated from the program, then from high school, and went on to work as a counselor for a young men's group in Brooklyn whose focus was developing community leaders through implementing wellness, wholeness, and mindful self-care practices with men. Jaylin later told Jozen, "I want to introduce them to what I learned about mindfulness, help them to see that as an option to cultivate resilience and tap into their innate capacities, to be heard, and to know when they're caught up in some harmful conditioning."

That first conversation opened the door to a journey of self-discovery and healing that Jaylin is now passing on to other young men in his community. It didn't start with Jozen trying to *teach* Jaylin anything or even speaking directly about the benefits of mindfulness or how it could help. It began with developing a real relationship, one based on authenticity, mutual respect, and trust. Jozen had the wisdom to leave some space, to just listen and connect on the human level. The relevance of mindfulness and a desire to learn more grew naturally out of their conversation and out of *embodying* mindfulness as much as *talking about* it.

Teaching mindfulness to adolescents is an art. It calls us to draw on all of our skills and faculties: our intelligence and creativity, our humanity, compassion, and humor. Success in this realm is tied to the development of three interrelated skill-sets: building authentic relationships, leaving space, and establishing personal relevance. In the best mindfulness instructions, these three go hand in hand, supporting one another in a fluid and seamless manner. We engage the kids in authentic conversation about what matters in their lives, making space to listen, building rapport, sowing seeds of trust, and learning *from them* how to speak to the ways in which this practice can be of benefit in their lives.

In this chapter, we will explore how the first two of these aims—building relationships and leaving space—work synergistically to create the conditions for young people to learn and practice mindfulness, sharing key tools for each. We'll discuss how your own authenticity, power-sharing ability, and genuine listening lay the groundwork for effective mindfulness teaching. We'll also examine how creating group agreements and using facilitation skills to spark discussion play a key role in teaching mindfulness to teens.

BUILDING AUTHENTIC RELATIONSHIPS

As educators, one of our primary tasks is to hone our interpersonal skills so that we can develop quality relationships of trust and mutual respect with the young folks we serve, with the purpose of fostering the growth of such relationships between and among students themselves. Such relationships are deeply nourishing for us human beings and especially so for teens and adolescents who often lack the unconditional acceptance, love, and affection for which they long. The more solid our rapport, the more risks the kids will take and the deeper they can go in their practice and their healing.

There are myriad ways to build such relationships, from how we show up in the room to how we co-create a group with students, from creatively integrating art or music to playing games or dancing. Within this wide field of options, finding your own authentic voice and way of connecting is perhaps the most essential. Young people have an incredibly sensitive internal meter for authenticity. As one high school teacher and mindfulness instructor noted in a conversation: "Teens can smell bullshit from anywhere." If you're putting on a front, trying to get their approval, or allowing your unresolved adolescent issues to take over, they'll pick up on it and lose interest. They'll either resist directly or avoid contact indirectly.

Bring your authentic self to the room. If you're being real, they'll recognize that and most likely be drawn to it. As we've explored, one of the most salient developmental features of this age is the process of differentiation and identity formation. Peer pressure, social anxiety, and insecurity are daily visitors. In a consumerist society, where happiness and self-worth are equated with material success, in a world of disembodied, disconnected, stressed-out adults, young people are *hungry* for authenticity. Given all of this, being at home in yourself is one of the most powerful things you can offer to teens. When you are authentic, it gives them permission to be themselves.

> **TRY THIS . . .**
>
> Organize students in pairs. Give each person three minutes to tell the other person about their family of origin, with the observer just listening. Then switch. Come back to the larger group and have each partner tell three things they learned about the other person. The kids love hearing that the other has really been listening and hearing their story through the words of their peer. Often you all learn things you may have never known about the student.

Develop your own language for teaching mindfulness that reflects your life experience and is appropriate to the context within which you teach. Incorporate what works from different sources (e.g., curricula, teachers, multimedia sources) while maintaining an uncompromising commitment to being yourself. Powerful teaching is the result of finding and refining our own unique voice and style. While you're teaching, pay attention to moments where you feel natural, moments where your physical posture and self-expression are in sync in such a way that you feel completely yourself. Take special note of those moments, letting the feeling of *naturalness* sink in. Use the wholehearted awareness of mindfulness practice to imprint that feeling in your consciousness so it becomes a reference point for your teaching.

Self-Disclosure

Authenticity is the language, the currency for working with adolescents. In this context, your ability to be real and vulnerable with others is a strength. Many educators find it helpful to share some of their own story early in the process of getting to know a class, often during the first session. Dave Smith, meditation teacher and educator, will give kids a 5-minute biography. "I tell them a little about my life. 'When I was your age, I had such-and-such trauma. I hated the world, hated my life, my parents . . . ' They're like, 'Me, too.' If you've been through something real, you can use that to build trust" (personal communication).

By sharing openly, the facilitator models strength through vulnerability, opens the door to a genuine relationship, and invites the kids to a deeper level of honesty. Self-disclosing can have a ripple effect. When done well, sharing your personal experience can build trust and safety and create an environment in which others are willing to take risks.

Enrique Collazo often begins Challenge Day (the anti-bullying and school community program) telling some of his own story of growing up around alcoholism in a poor, violent neighborhood in Los Angeles:

> I had it worse than some, better than others. The city was chaotic. By 11 years old, I was already having thoughts of suicide—a child in so much pain, with no healthy strategies, not wanting or willing to feel. At 13, I joined a gang. I was confused, using drugs and alcohol, and doing the best I could to survive with the tools I had. Looking back I can see I was just trying to protect myself. I didn't want to get hurt . . . Whether or not they can relate to those conditions (some do, but a lot of them don't), they understand the emotions. They know what it's like to feel lonely, to be dealing with pain and heaviness in unhealthy ways, to numb out. There's something about my willingness to be vulnerable with them, about witnessing the capacity to have some emotional intelligence, that gives them a glimpse that things could be different for them. (personal interview)

There are many creative ways to invite students to express themselves authentically. In one of the signature activities for Challenge Day, the facilitator draws an image of an iceberg. A small peak pokes out above sea level, while the bulk of the iceberg lies hidden below the surface. They discuss the metaphor: How much do we show who we really are here at school? How much remains invisible, hiding below the surface? They explore what makes it hard to be authentic at school, the fears of being judged or excluded, and invite the possibility of "dropping the water line" to expose the rest of the iceberg and reveal more of who they are. What does it take to create a space together where they don't have to be scared, where they can let their guard down, take a risk to be vulnerable, and be themselves?

When we've done our job well, created the proper conditions of safety and trust and given teens permission to be real, they have the capacity to take enormous emotional risks. Many educators (ourselves included) feel regularly inspired by their raw authenticity, their willingness to share openly and unabashedly. Morris Ervin recounts the transformation of one very quiet student, a young man whose brother had been killed by the police. He rarely said a word in high school. At the talent show at the end of Morris' 3-month mentoring program, he was dancing and reciting poetry on stage, in front of the whole school.

Creating the conditions for this kind of open sharing requires a level of vulnerability that a lot of adults don't feel comfortable with in general, let alone with teens and adolescents. It requires walking a fine line between sharing openly and maintaining appropriate boundaries. The danger of sharing too much is that we take center stage, make the relationship about our own needs, or collapse the differentiation of roles into becoming friends. On the other hand, if we don't share any of our vulnerability and hold the role too rigidly or opaquely, we limit the possibilities for learning and connection.

While powerful, self-disclosure must be done consciously and intentionally, with an awareness of how it will serve. Different levels of self-disclosure are appropriate for different environments. Educators, mental health professionals, and mentors are trained to disclose personal life experiences carefully, with the primary aim always to serve the students rather than our own interests. We don't self-disclose because we want to get something off our chest or to seek attention from adolescents.

Strategic disclosure builds connection and models a fluid, dynamic relationship to power. By sharing personally, we can demonstrate that we're not holding too tightly to the authority of our role. (At the same time, this can be overused as a way of disavowing the power we do hold—and need to hold to—in our role.) If you feel drawn to disclose something personal, check your intention. Are you doing it because it will benefit the youth? Or are you doing this to get approval, be liked, or mask fear? As soon as the intention shifts to serving our own ends rather than the youth, disclosing may be counterproductive.

Showing Genuine Interest and Empathy

One of the most valuable gifts we can give to one another is the experience of being seen. For human beings, some of our most core psychological needs center around relationship: feeling connected, being understood, belonging, and knowing that we matter. Genuine human connection and attunement is increasingly lacking in our fast-paced, modern digital world. Yet it is something that children and youth long for and depend on for their development—and something we can offer freely when we are present in a balanced way.

What does it take to really see our students? To create the space in our own mind to have a true encounter with another human being? We must be willing to slow down a little and look with fresh eyes. Can we set aside our lingering irritations from yesterday? Can we hold the lesson plan a bit more lightly and relax into being here together, right now?

For some students, especially for kids who have gone through a lot, our ability to simply show up each week in a consistent and reliable manner speaks volumes. Bart van Melik reflected on his own realization of how essential this was in *Still, in the City* (2018). He writes:

The other week, I had to do an evaluation at the juvenile detention center and so they had to fill out a questionnaire. And one question was, "What do you like about the meditation program?" One girl just said, "Bart." And I asked, "Why?" She said, "You're always there. Just the fact that you show up and we can come together as a group." That is key. (p. 84)

Being in the room itself is a powerful statement of our commitment to the kids. The quality of our presence and taking an active interest in their lives goes two steps further, inviting students to feel how they matter.

Genuine interest is one of the qualities young people crave most; it confers the reassurance of being loved and accepted unconditionally for who they are. Many are under extreme pressure—from family, teachers, peers, or society in general—to conform to preconceived ideas about who and how they should be by a certain age. Whether it's the pressure of high academic achievement, or the pain of having no one believe in you and being told (directly or indirectly) that you won't amount to much, adolescence often includes an external demand to shut off who you are and become what others expect you to be. Part of the role of the mindfulness instructor is to embody the capacity to listen and care in a nonjudgmental way. Instead of being another adult who is trying to change or fix them or make them better, you just hold space for them to feel what's present and discover what's true inside.

This is supported by developing our capacities for empathy and attunement. Empathy is the overall capacity to *feel into* others' experience, the ability to see things from their perspective and to join them with felt understanding. Attunement is the connectedness, the resonance of empathy. It's our ability to intuitively sense and mirror another's internal state kinesthetically and emotionally. Our hearts, minds, and bodies begin to synchronize, like the vibration of two strings in harmony. Here's Enrique Collazo again: "I'm not a natural public speaker, I'm not even a teen person. I'm pretty awkward and unsure around teens outside of work. I don't know much about pop culture and all things teen . . . What draws kids in is my ability to attune to them, to be super compassionate and loving. I listen and I see them; they're hungry for that."

Susan, a high school art teacher, recounts the experience of sitting down to speak with a freshman, Avery. Though normally quite bubbly and cheerful, Avery had been behaving unusually and looking down. When they began talking Avery mentioned dropping out of school, Susan noticed her old habits rushing in: *fix this, rescue Avery, solve the problem.* She paused and decided to try offering empathy instead. "Tell me more. What's going on?" As Susan listened, Avery began to open up. She was being bullied. She felt sad, alone, and depressed. Tears began to flow; Susan continued to listen. There were awkward silences, when Avery lingered with a questioning look on her face as if to say, "Is this okay? Can I go on?" Susan held her gaze, from time to time reflecting what she was hearing, asking a clarifying question, or just nodding. Whenever she noticed the desire to go into fix-it mode she would restrain the impulse.

The conversation deepened, until Avery realized she'd felt this way since early elementary school. "Was that the first time you felt so sad and alone?" No, the first time was even earlier—during her preschool years—when her father had left home. They stopped and looked at each other, recognizing that they'd hit the root of her painful feelings of isolation. Eventually they talked about what was next and discussed plans to address the bullying. Avery decided to share her experiences with others with an art project on depression. This is the power of listening with empathy. What would have happened if Susan hadn't been mindful enough to restrain her habit of offering advice? Where might the conversation have ended if she had jumped to strategies right away and tried to convince Avery to stay in school?

Attune to your kids, sensing their current state and what they need. *This won't work if it's a technique or intervention.* It must be a genuine expression of your own deep interest in knowing who they are. Aim to meet them with a spirit of openness and care, which will build trust and can catalyze healing.

Forest Fein, educator and founder of the mindfulness program, Wise Up, says the following about this aspect of working with adolescents:

> I allow myself to be moved by and deeply care for these kids. It's so inspiring to see the resiliency of the human spirit. What some of these kids have gone through is hard to fathom . . . yet they're these amazing human beings with so much potential. If you create the right conditions, they start to blossom. Most of them didn't have the love and support that any human being needs to thrive. So a lot of our work is about creating the conditions that allow their potential to come forward. It's like they're these beautiful plants that haven't had enough sun or water, and have been planted in barren soil. Then we start to shine the light of care and compassion on them, we fertilize the soil with kindness, with these teachings and practices, and over time you can watch them open up and become more healthy, vibrant beings (personal communication).

Part of the healing potential of empathic attunement comes from the key role it plays in developing secure attachment bonding in human development. Psychiatrist and psychoanalyst John Bowlby defined healthy attachment as lasting psychological connectedness between human beings (1969/2008). His formative theory suggests that our ability to engage in and maintain healthy relationships depends in part on a template forged through early experience with our parents or primary caregivers. When there is a legacy of loss or pain, the relational template can be repaired through a surrogate relationship later in life where the qualities of healthy attachment are present. Indeed, one of the strongest predictors for successful outcomes in psychotherapy is the *therapeutic alliance* between the therapist and client. Understanding the facets of this kind of empathic relationship are important for working with adolescents, many of whom are lacking such key formative experiences with adults.

In a secure, healthy attachment, the parent figure provides the following qualities:

- A balance of **safety and protection** without being overbearing, allowing the child space to explore while still looking after them.
- A keen **attunement** to the child's development changes, emotions, and overall internal state of being. This includes empathy, mirroring, and validating their affect.
- The ability to **comfort and soothe** the child when they are in distress.
- The capacity to inspire **healthy self-esteem** by repeatedly expressing joy in relation to the child's being, rather than solely in their actions or accomplishments.
- A willingness to offer **support and encouragement** of the child's best self-development, discovering their unique identity rather than having an agenda or preconceived idea of who this person should be. (Brown & Elliot, 2016)

Although these capacities for empathy and attunement are innate, we face many barriers to developing this quality, both collectively and individually. Modern society's value on individualism tends to highlight our separateness, while western civilization's emphasis on cognitive intelligence tends to devalue empathy and emotional intelligence. Society's focus on efficiency and the tendency toward busyness coupled with technology's reduction in face-to-face contact leaves less time for connection. Gender roles and the socialization process can warp our understanding of empathy, writing it off as *soft* or *weak,* or forcing it upon us as a *selfless duty.* As educators in regular contact with adolescents, we have the opportunity to become the supportive adults our most vulnerable students need.

Mindfulness practice, when done properly, is an essential support for developing empathy. The practice makes us genuinely curious about inner and outer reality, cultivates care, and strengthens a deep capacity for listening even in the face of intensity. Ground your teaching and facilitation in an active curiosity about the lived experience of your students. Learn to ask open-ended questions and to actively reflect what you're hearing (Walsh & Sattes, 2011). Listen and really try to understand. Look at your kids and make an effort to see their faces, their eyes, and their expressions. True curiosity is not a teaching strategy. It is a result of having a fresh, innocent, and vulnerable relationship with the world on a moment-by-moment basis.

Cultivate patience, which is an important internal support for listening with empathy. Finally, as we've already mentioned, self-care, community, and a strong peer support network are often necessary to increase our capacities for empathy and attunement. When we feel seen, heard, and nourished, it's easier to offer that space to others.

GIVING ADOLESCENTS SPACE

At the heart of listening with empathy is a central principle in teaching mindfulness to adolescents: we aim to give them space to explore their inner world and share with one another, rather than imparting knowledge from us to them. Leaving space and supporting peer-to-peer learning can be unfamiliar and at times uncomfortable if we have been trained to view our role as teachers quite differently. Yet, as we'll see, some of the most transformative and richest moments of learning come not from us, but from the teens themselves.

Khalila Gillett Archer, former program director of iBme, shares the story of an adolescent with autism who attended several teen meditation retreats (personal communication). At the first retreat, his mom stayed nearby, uncertain how things would go. The teen was extraordinarily shy, clinging to her, not wanting to be in the group. He would participate some in group activities, testing the waters, appearing uncomfortable and staying very contained. Khalila and the staff created space for him to show up to the degree that he was willing, making it clear that his degree of participation was completely up to him. The next year he came back. And the next. By his third retreat, during the community sharing on the final night, he danced in front of everyone. Some present were in tears. Everyone understood the significance of the kind of trust it took him to open up in that way.

These kinds of stories happen regularly for skilled mindfulness educators, but only because they make space for the youth to be themselves, trusting each young person's individual unfolding. This is made possible by a powerful core principle at the heart of this work with adolescents: rather than transmit knowledge or information, give them space to explore their inner world and share with one another.

If you hold the attitude that's so pervasive in our educational institutions—"I'm the teacher and I have something important you need to learn"—be prepared for an uphill battle. That very attitude reinforces the power relations teens face every day, a dynamic that all too often refuses to see them for who they are. Rather than putting anything *in* to teens, the aim is to give them space to let stuff *out*! We create a space in which they can unload thoughts and emotions, where they can talk about the fear, anxiety, pain, and confusion they've been holding inside.

In order to offer the kind of space where teens can be themselves, share openly, and explore, you must learn to hold power and authority in a conscious, skillful manner. This requires both a sense of innate confidence in your own ability to take up space and use your authority when necessary and the capacity to tolerate any discomfort and uncertainty as you let go enough to allow things to unfold organically.

At the heart of good work with adolescents is the view of mutual respect and a radical departure from society's preconceived roles and hierarchies in favor of authentic human connection. The nature of the relationship is one of mentoring: an authentic connection with an adult who doesn't have an agenda and isn't an authority figure, but who has valuable life experience to share. For millennia in human culture (as well as to this day in traditional societies), such role models and mentors were readily available in the extended family, the village, or the community. Teaching mindfulness and working with adolescents opens the door to reestablishing such vital connections.

Jessica Morey of Inward Bound Mindfulness Education (iBme) talks about this importance of not placing oneself above the kids or assuming that we know more. "We have to be willing to have a real relationship. I don't see myself as putting skills into their minds. I'm just bringing out what's already in them." In a similar fashion, Fein, of Wise Up, shares, "Part of it is just allowing myself to care about another human being . . . I try to meet them as equals, as fellow human beings, while at the same time providing the necessary guidance and structure to gain their respect. But so much of that respect actually comes from relating to them as equals."

Morris Ervin calls it "youth choice and voice," pointing to how rarely young adults have the experience of choice or feel heard. From the very beginning, we can establish a framework that this is *their* time, *their* program; we can draw out what matters most to them. In creating that space, the very container for teaching mindfulness highlights their ability to choose and capitalizes upon their developmentally heightened need for autonomy.

Strategies for Sharing Power

How you offer this space is all about finding your own authentic way; it's part of what makes teaching mindfulness to adolescents such a creative and invigorating process. One common approach is to place more emphasis at first on listening than speaking. Here's Dave Smith, a long-time mindfulness educator: "If I start out talking *at them*, I'm recreating the same old paradigm." Instead of starting with a whole introduction, he'll flip the script by hanging back a little, waiting, watching, and being receptive to them. "What happens if I'm present in the room, just hanging out in a relaxed way with no agenda? They don't know what to do with that, it throws them off-guard. I'm already modeling something and presenting a new option from the get-go: you don't have to be an uptight adult."

Another strategy for creating space is to engage in a shared activity. Jozen Tamori Gibson talks about the important of hanging out with the young people who come to Brooklyn Zen Center. "We've got a kitchen where we'll just cook, listen to music, get to know one another. It can seem like it's surface level, but it's not. When we're sharing and having a natural, organic conversation we're building trust. Even if I say, 'This is a place you can be open and feel free to express yourself,' it takes time to develop that trust, so you have to be patient."

How you use language is another important way to signal our interest in honoring their autonomy and sharing power. Young people are given commands and told what to do all day long from almost every adult in their life. The skilled mindfulness educator is able to stimulate interest by giving them choices. Rather than stating orders, use words that extend invitations, ask questions, or make suggestions. For example: "Here are some ideas . . . You don't have to do this, but check it out if you want . . . .Maybe we could . . . ? How about we . . . ? What do you think about . . . ? I invite you to. . . " Stay alert to any tendency to use your authority in the room to attempt to dictate, control, or manipulate their behavior rather than to invite their genuine engagement. (For more on working with resistance, see below).

As Smith points out, when you use language in this way you're implicitly doing two things. First, you're introducing a choice, which is innately disarming. Second, you're beginning with a contemplative framework, inviting the students to *consider* something, asking them to *check this out*. Already, you're shifting their attention to a more reflective mode. The framing itself is part of the teaching.

All of these strategies (as well as the range of others we discuss below), rest on an inner orientation of genuine interest, patience, sensitivity, and attunement. Together with the longing to be seen and heard and to express themselves, most teens come with a sense of skepticism or tentativeness, wondering "How will I be received? Can I really be myself here?" Leaving space relationally, in the conversation and environment, depends on our ability to create space internally, within ourselves. That internal space is what allows us to receive another human being.

Here one relies on bringing the inner qualities of mindfulness practice out into the relationship—the potency of compassionate, wholehearted listening. The genuineness of your inquiry, your willingness to pause and wait, is a key part of leaving space for young people to come forward and express themselves. Part of the work of the educator is to look at young people with fresh eyes and see their potential. Beneath the posturing, the aloofness, the acting out or goofing off, can you discern that their hearts are longing to shine? Can you hold that possibility for them even when they can't see it for themselves?

CREATING A CONTAINER

Another key aspect of giving space to young people is establishing a safe *container*—a sense of being held and safe physically as well as psychologically and emotionally. Aim to create an environment that feels welcoming, structured enough that young folks can relax, yet flexible enough to allow spontaneity and creative exploration.

Perhaps most essential for this are the relational skills we've been exploring, which lay the foundation. A container also includes the physical space of your program. Do everything you can to set the room up in a way that you anticipate will help students feel at ease. This might mean setting up chairs in a circle or informal arrangement rather than rows or even procuring relevant artwork or more comfortable seating like couches, if possible. Experiment with adjusting the lighting or playing music in the background.

A key consideration in creating the container is whether you co-teach, team teach, or lead solo. Many mindfulness programs favor co-facilitating, which can bring more representative, diverse leadership in terms of gender identity, ethnicity, sexual orientation, and other aspects of personal identity.

Having leaders with different voices and life experiences can be incredibly important for adolescents who are actively exploring their own identity.

Teaching with a co-facilitator also gives you a wider pool of wisdom and creativity to draw on, providing key benefits in both teaching and classroom management. One person can take the lead in a discussion while the other steps back and observes, trading off as needed. In handling behavior issues, team teaching enhances creativity and opens up the option for more one-to-one attention when needed. With all team teaching, ensure that the relationship between you and your co-facilitator is solid. Spend time getting to know another. Be sure to discuss your approach to teaching, as well as any expectations, agreements, or requests you might have about how you'd like to work together and support each other.

With all of these suggestions, orient toward creating a sense of group cohesion and a feeling of togetherness. Making this a priority will have an effect on how you show up and how things unfold. Again, here's van Melik: "If I'm just meeting them where they are, we might end up having a long conversation about inspirational figures in our lives. And we all walk away highly inspired. We didn't do any stretching, we didn't do any meditating, but we formed a group."

Group Agreements

As we explored when discussing teen retreats, an essential component of creating a container is establishing community agreements that function as guidelines for how you engage with one another. The generation of these agreements is a wonderful opportunity to get creative and engage your kids. You can do team-building exercises that involve movement and build trust, play a game that requires cooperation, or engage the group in honest conversation. To increase safety and buy-in and to differentiate the environment from other settings where power is held in an authoritarian manner, clinician and educator Sam Himelstein (2013) suggests beginning these conversations by discussing the difference between rules and agreements. Rules are enforced by punishment; agreements invite a relationship and conversation.

Some instructors like to introduce a set of core agreements or principles as a proposal and then tweak them with each particular group, while others prefer to craft them collaboratively with the kids. Introducing a predetermined set of guidelines can be helpful if you have limited time with a group, while co-creating them can be a powerful way to establish buy-in and a sense of ownership. Himelstein suggests the following core agreements as a starting place, defining them together as a group:

+ Respect (for self and others)
+ "One mic" (not talking when someone is talking)
+ Skillful speech and skillful listening

When introducing predetermined guidelines, frame them as a suggestion and ask for agreement, rather than presenting them as rules. "Here are some things that might make our time together more meaningful, that I'd like you to consider. While I'm here, I'd like to ask you to . . . Does that work for you?" If discussing agreements collaboratively, invite your students to consider a question that gets at the terrain, either asking explicitly, "What kinds of agreements do we want to make for how we're going to be with each other?" or suggesting something more broadly, like "What helps you to feel relaxed in a group?" or "What does respect mean to you?"

In creating agreements, it's essential to discuss the intention behind them so that they don't become another set of rules superimposed by adults. Help the teens make the connection between these agreements and how they want to be treated themselves. Why or how would this be valuable to you? One innovative way to devise group agreements is to talk about the reality of their lives. What's it like at home, at school, or out on the street? How does it feel to have peer pressure around sex or drugs, to always be on guard or to have watch your back? The instructor can then hold out the possibility of another way of being: What would it be like if things were different here? How would it feel to be able to relax some and *not* have to watch your back? Such questions empower the young people to create the space by inviting them to imagine it together.

The actual agreements you create can range from more traditional ones like, "respect yourself, respect each other, speak from your own experience . . ." to more playful or reflective ones. One of Jozen's favorites is "Don't yuck my yum," pointing to the intention to honor each individual's need to celebrate and find joy in unique ways. Another, more reflective guideline he uses at BZC is encouraging young folks to practice holding an awareness of "both/and." This guideline is an invitation to remember that someone else's reality is as beautiful and important as one's own; difference becomes an invitation to conversation and learning rather than a sign of separation.

These agreements themselves can begin to create a sense of cohesion, that we're all in this together. They're meant to act as a framework for building authentic relationships and to address the reality of the challenges that are likely to come up in the group. Be careful not to have too many agreements (which become hard to remember or follow) and to avoid creating double standards between the young people and the facilitators. Your ability to model the group's agreements in a natural way can inspire the kids to see their value.

In crafting agreements it's also essential to be realistic—both about the limits of one's ability to create safety, and the fact that agreements may be broken. Some educators make the mistake of saying, "This is a safe space; you can be yourself here," without recognizing the false promise in saying that. Safety is a myth. The world is not a safe place—physically or emotionally, and we can't actually guarantee anyone's safety. Sometimes, the very assertion of safety may work counter to your intentions. What we can do is have a clear intention and set about taking steps to produce that outcome, while understanding that we can't make anyone feel completely free from danger.

Whatever agreements you make, be sure to include some discussion about how to handle things when an agreement is broken. Whose responsibility is it to name a deviation from group norms? How is it handled? How we recreate the container when someone breaks an agreement is an essential aspect of building trust, deepening relationships, and modeling emotional maturity. Breaking agreements can vary widely depending on the context: from a sharp comment to physical aggression in an after-school program, to someone smoking pot or making out on a teen retreat. The actions you take will depend on the context, and how you respond internally is where that begins. Take the same care in mending a broken agreement that you took in creating it. Can you come from a place of compassion and understanding, rather than being punitive or demoralizing or demonizing someone because they made a mistake? The aim is to respond appropriately and attempt to reestablish connection, while modeling setting healthy limits and engaging in repair.

We've found some particular agreements helpful. The adolescents who tend to be more vocal can practice stepping back and making room for others. Those who are hesitant or shy can practice stepping up and sharing their voice. Listening patiently and mindfully without speaking over others is important in some settings. Being conscious of the difference between one's intention and the impact that one's words has on others is one way we can tend to the group atmosphere and foster a sense of belonging. Bring an attitude of curiosity to each other.

CONSIDER THIS . . .

Making an agreement regarding confidentiality can be tricky given the vulnerable memories that mindfulness can bring to the surface and our responsibilities as mandated reporters. Be sure to let your kids know what the line is for you so that they don't feel betrayed if there is something that needs to be reported. As for times when the students communicate

*with each other, confidentiality should have very clear lines
so that a level of confidence and trust can be created in the
mindfulness setting.*

Routines

A final aspect of the container is employing some kind of structure for your classes. This begins with the moment students arrive. Consciously greet them, being sure to make eye contact or appropriate physical gestures depending on the setting—a handshake, a fist bump, perhaps a hug. Many instructors will use a secular ritual to begin and end their mindfulness sessions, which helps students recognize the shift to a more intentional space and settle in. This could be anything from ringing a bell to reciting a poem or short dedication.

Meditation teacher Bart van Melik uses a three-part structure as the core of his classes in New York City (personal communication). Each class begins with a group contemplation, exploring a universal theme, often using a talking stick in council format (in which an object is passed around the circle and only the person holding the talking piece speaks while all others listen). The second phase of the class brings that theme into a visceral experience through mindful movement. The last phase takes the theme into an inward, contemplative experience through mindfulness practice.

For example, van Melik might begin a lesson introducing the concept of trust, pointing out a common tattoo among the teens he teaches, "Trust No One." He'll pose a question: "Is there someone you trust in your life 100%? Yes or no, and why?" Young folks share, one at a time, unpacking what trust means, how it's present or absent in their lives. Then, he'll offer some simple yoga balancing poses, inviting the kids to explore trusting their body to balance. Finally, he might lead some mindfulness of breathing, inviting them to question: "Do you trust your body's ability to breath? Do you trust mindfulness, being aware?"

Morris Ervin prefers to begin his classes with music or a game to help lighten the atmosphere and get kids in their bodies. Then he'll introduce an intention or theme to discuss and proceed from there. The particular content of the structure is less important than the fact of its predictability.

When there is a set map to follow, kids can relax because they know where they are in the routine and what to expect. This can be particularly helpful when working with young folks who have experienced trauma. In these circumstances, providing a regular structure supports the students' ability to feel safe and relax, creating the conditions for more meaningful interactions and a richer exploration of the mindfulness activities.

CHAPTER 5

ESTABLISHING RELEVANCE AND FOSTERING GROUP ENGAGEMENT

In one particular class in a Manhattan high school, the instructor, Bart, had noticed a shift over time to more and more mutual respect. He felt compelled to do some relational work in dyads and invited a series of reflections on judgment: "What judgments do you have about school? About teachers? And finally, what judgments do you have about yourself?" By the third round the room was still and quiet. While unpacking the activity in the large group, one young man put his hand on his heart and said, "It might sound really weird, but I never knew that you all judged yourself. I feel really happy to know I'm not the only one judging myself." There was a long moment of silence, a sort of deep, communal nod with appreciation for his willingness to say something they were all feeling.

BUILDING RELATIONSHIPS OF MUTUAL RESPECT, leaving space, and creating a safe container (discussed in Chapter 4), go a long way toward developing rapport and trust with young people. The mindfulness instructor must also be able to frame the importance of mindfulness and give adolescents an entry point to the practice that makes sense. You must answer the implicit question: "Why should I pay attention to you and try this? What's in it for me?" If there's no buy-in—if you don't provide a context and show its relevance for their actual lived experience—you're just another adult in the room talking. You're likely to be met with an attitude of "whatever. . . ."

In this chapter, we'll share key tools for establishing the relevance of mindfulness, from storytelling and metaphor to mixed-media and personal anecdote. We'll also explore how to build creatively on a sense of personal connection to create an experience of engagement and inquiry among adolescents.

MAKING MINDFULNESS RELEVANT FOR ADOLESCENTS

One of the main tasks of a mindfulness instructor is to pique the curiosity of young people, to stimulate interest and authentic engagement with mindfulness practice. In fact, curiosity is at the heart of this practice. When mindfulness practitioners become genuinely interested in their inner lives, a whole new dimension of practice opens up. They no longer rely on extrinsic forces for motivation. In seminal work on motivation, Ryan and Deci (2000) distinguish between two types of motivation: intrinsic motivation, doing something because it is inherently interesting or rewarding, versus extrinsic motivation, doing something because it leads to a separate outcome. They write:

> [There is a] critical distinction between behaviors that are volitional and accompanied by the experience of freedom and autonomy—those that emanate from one's sense of self—and those that are accompanied by the experience of pressure and control and are not representative of one's self. Intrinsically motivated behaviors, which are performed out of interest and satisfy the innate psychological needs for competence and autonomy are the prototype of self-determined behavior. Extrinsically motivated behaviors—those that are executed because they are instrumental to some separable consequence—can vary in the extent to which they represent self-determination. (p. 65)

Mindfulness can be fueled by extrinsic motivation for some time, for example, the desire to follow an adult's recommendation or to achieve some particular outcome from the practice. However, this is not a durable source of motivation. The intrinsic rewards of curious exploration are vital ingredients in the path of practice.

Students connect to mindfulness in different ways, so relying on a single curriculum or manual, no matter how comprehensive, often will be insufficient. Rather, you must have a variety of different material to engage youth—activities, themes, short lessons, stories, and examples. One particular description of mindfulness may be compelling for one student but uninspiring for another. As one angle wears out, you must become skilled at effortlessly replacing it with another or challenging the class to reengage with the original theme. This is the art of teaching adolescents.

The Hook

At the core of creating relevance is ability to help kids make conceptual connections between their life and mindfulness, essentially relating "something I know and care about" to "something I don't know." This is often done through the use of a *hook*. A hook is an organizing concept that draws the listener in, that you can return to again and again to orient the group to mindfulness. Jae Pasari teaches a course on concentration techniques called "Jedi Mind Control" at a public charter high school in California, in which the hook centers around a Star Wars analogy. The course bears the following description, which highlights not only the core hook but the promise of its benefits: "*Harness The Force to improve your concentration and awareness skills with ancient contemplative practices. Side effects may include improved academic and athletic performance, increased happiness, flow states, and general awesomeness*" (Bissanti, Brown, & Pasari, 2019).

Chris McKenna suggests the analogy that "the mind is like a car" (2015). McKenna's list below illustrates how this one simple hook can create relevance, meaning, and cohesion over many lessons. Each point can be drawn out to make further connections through a discussion, activity, or lesson, leading into formal mindfulness exercises:

- A car has an owner's manual. This mindfulness class is like an owner's manual for your mind.
- Cars are only safe if the brakes work. Mindfulness is like learning how to apply the brakes in our life. What happens when we're going too fast?
- Cars are only useful if you can steer. Mindfulness helps us learn how to make better choices and steer in our life.
- Cars need maintenance. What happens if you don't change the oil or put more gas in? Our mind, body, and nervous system are the same. Mindfulness, kindness, and the other things you'll learn in this class are core tools for taking care of yourself. They're free, don't require any special gear, can be done anytime, and don't rely on other people.
- Cars have gears, so does your mind. "Reverse, Neutral, and Drive" are like the past, present, and future. If we get stuck in any one gear we're in trouble. Mindfulness helps us learn how to shift gears and let go of thoughts or feelings.

In order for it to work, a hook must be relevant to that particular community of young people. For instance, a car analogy might fall flat in a setting where kids rely on trains and buses. Here is a short list of ideas for analogies that might resonate with your students. See what sparks your imagination; create your own metaphor for your group.

- **Advanced technology:** If you went back in time 100 years and gave someone a laptop or smartphone, would they know how to use it? You've been given the most advanced piece of technology on the planet: a human mind and body. How well do you know how to use it? This class is like having a user guide that can teach you how to understand the hardware, how to detect and remove viruses and malware, how to upgrade the operating system, and even how to create your own software program.

+ **Friendship:** Engage in a discussion about the value of friendship. What does it mean to be a good friend? How do you know if someone really cares about you? Are they checking their phone when you're talking with them, or are they giving you their undivided attention? How does it feel to spend time with a good friend? Practicing mindfulness is like learning to be your own good friend, to have your own back.

+ **Mental hygiene:** We clean our teeth and our body every day. What would it be like if you stopped brushing your teeth or bathing? How often do you clean your heart and mind? Do you know how to clear out the gunk when you get stressed or angry or down?

+ **Mental training:** We can train our bodies in many different ways: athletics, exercise, music, art. Why don't we train our minds? How could it help you if mindfulness is mind training?

+ **Intelligence:** Have you ever been told that you're smart? That you're not smart? Are you street smart? There are lots of kinds of intelligence, not just academic intelligence: emotional intelligence, body (kinesthetic) intelligence. Traditional education teaches us *what* to think, but not how to think and learn. Because mindfulness helps us train our attention, it is a foundation for learning lots of other things; it is a kind of intelligence.

+ **Training a puppy:** The mind is like a puppy—always running and darting from one place to another. If a puppy is cooped up in a small room, it might get especially wild. Mindfulness is like giving the puppy a big lawn to run around freely. Eventually, it will settle down.

+ **Focus:** If you want to make a sketch you need a sharp pencil. Mindfulness is a tool that makes your mind sharp. What can you do with a sharp mind?

+ **Self-discovery:** What does a master key do? It opens any door. Mindfulness is like having a master key for your mind: it can open any door and let you understand what's inside. What doors would you open in yourself if you had a master key?

+ **Microscope and understanding:** What's a microscope do? The ordinary mind is like looking through a microscope that is out of focus or shaking. Through mindfulness training, we steady and focus our inner vision to see things more clearly. What happens when we see things more clearly? We can understand them. What would you want to understand more in yourself?

+ **Dignity and purpose:** A dog will chase any old bone you throw to it, no matter where or how far you throw it. A lion will sit back and watch. Our minds can be like that dog, chasing after every thought or feeling. Mindfulness teaches us how to be like a regal lion, the king of the jungle who is steady, unafraid, and focused on its purpose.

+ **Autonomy:** How much choice do you feel you have in your life? Does it feel as if adults have been telling you what to do since you were young? "Eat this. Don't eat that. Do your homework. Clean your room." Autonomy means being your own ruler, your own governor. Mindfulness helps us discover an autonomy inside that no one can take away.

+ **Standing up to thoughts:** Whatever thought comes up in our mind, we tend to believe it and act on it. We've been bossed around by our thoughts our entire life. Mindfulness gives us the strength to stand up to bossy thoughts. Are you going to be bossed around by your thoughts forever?

+ **Muddy water:** Thoughts and feelings are like mud in a glass of water that's been stirred up. Mindfulness practice allows the mud to settle to the bottom of the glass, so that the water is clear.

+ **The sky:** Awareness is like the sky. There is space in the sky for everything. Thoughts and feelings drift through like clouds, but the sky is undisturbed. So too, worries and sorrow and joy drift through awareness, but awareness isn't defined by what drifts through. As our minds settle, even the clouds themselves start to appear more like the sky.

As you can see, the possibilities are endless. Linguists like George Lakoff consider metaphor a fundamental mechanism of the mind, suggesting that humans live by metaphors. "New metaphors are capable of creating new understandings and, therefore, new realities" (Lakoff & Johnson, 2008, p. 235). The secret of a good hook is relating it to the specific context within which you are working in a way that is dynamic and gets students' attention. It has to mean something to them and speak to their world, their lived experience, a pain point, or something they want more of in their lives.

Making Connections

The first meeting with a group of teens is perhaps the most important. If you have that opportunity to start fresh (rather than leading a drop-in group), make the most of it—we can never make a first impression twice. Weave together the tools and perspectives we've discussed: be authentic, create group agreements, and choose a theme that you feel confident will work. Create enough relevance so that they want to give it a try; then provide an experience of mindfulness early on so they have a taste of it.

The beautiful part about establishing relevance is that your students can help you make the connections to their lives if you give them an opportunity to do so. Many educators who work with teens will confess with amusement, "I'm not that hip and don't pretend to be!" Invite the students to tell you, "Who are the people that inspire you in your life? Where do you struggle?" Charisse Minerva teaches mindfulness on teen retreats with iBme as well as in schools and local communities in Virginia. She explains, "It takes a level of humility to recognize that we have something to learn from each other. I like to draw them out, to bring their own stories into the room. I can introduce a topic, pose a question about their lives and then let them teach me" (personal communication).

Morris Ervin points out that it doesn't have to be that deep to get kids interested. "You have to give them something to connect with. Engage them on the surface based on *their* interests. Kids like music, they like fashion . . . I do my homework. I'm constantly learning what they like." Ervin will ask the kids to make him a mix, or set up a mic and some speakers in the cafeteria to play music and take requests, so that by the end of one lunch period he leaves with 30–40 songs to explore. Rather than pretending to share their interests, his curiosity and enthusiasm helps create genuine points of connection.

> **TRY THIS . . .**
>
> These are the shoes of someone who. This is a group exercise (game) where the group stands in a circle. One person at a time puts their shoes in the middle of the circle and says to the group, "these are the shoes of someone who . . . . . ." here is the opportunity for the participant to tell something about themselves that they are willing for the group to know about them. Once everyone has gone, one person at a time the shoes are returned to the people who placed them by saying again, "these are the shoes of someone who. . . . ." and the participant, who is not the shoe owner reports back to the shoe owner the words they said about themselves.

You also can foster relevance by bringing in role models from history or popular culture and connecting them to qualities of mindfulness, an aspect of the practice, or a situation in their lives. Minerva says, "I intentionally bring in famous people who use mindfulness or embody some quality we're learning about: sports athletes, musicians. I'm also really sensitive whenever giving a presentation to always use pictures and quotes from figures that represent the people in the room, whether it's Martin Luther King Jr., Gandhi, or Jay-Z."

Many educators will do some version of an activity where they ask young folks to bring in a favorite song or lyric and then discuss its meaning in their life. Ervin invites students to play a 30-second clip of a song that fits their struggles or defines their identity and then to talk about why. Minerva points out that there's often a lot more going on in the songs than adults may realize. She recounts one teen explaining that the lead singer's brother had died from an opioid overdose and the song was about the role the pharmaceutical industry plays in causing addiction. If you've done the groundwork to build a relationship and you ask students what's important to them, they'll tell you.

Integrating other disciplines is another way to generate interest and make the practice come alive. Young people often love learning about the brain, which can help to depersonalize difficult experiences like anxiety, fear, or obsessive thinking. Effective adult mindfulness teachers often have training across different fields (neurobiology, mythology, psychology, or another field) in order to make their teachings relevant to their students. What other information can you weave into your teaching to enrich the content in a way that is interesting to youth?

Another creative strategy to engage the class is to teach a lesson, and then invite them to create their own version of the lesson and teach it back to their peers. Calling it a "teach back," Minerva shares how creative students have been with these peer-led lessons. In a mindful eating teach-back, one group of students used jawbreakers, talking about the many layers of an experience; another used crunchy hot Cheetos and Kool-Aid. "By the end of it, their classmates were reading the ingredients on the back of the bag to figure out why it tastes this way, and what is red dye #5?" It turned into a wider exploration because they had the freedom to create their own lesson, relevant to their own lives.

A skilled educator is also able to use any of the strategies for building relationship and creating space that we've already discussed to create relevance. For example, after playing any kind of game or warm-up activity, debrief the activity with pointed questions that help students tie their experience back to mindfulness. If you've just done a silent count-off (challenge students to count to twenty in no particular order, with no other communication, starting over any time two people speak at the same time, forcing everyone to attune to everyone else) discuss what worked and what didn't work, highlighting innate qualities that are related to mindfulness like patience, listening, and attunement. Segue into a discussion about how those qualities could be useful in the rest of their lives, and how mindfulness techniques help to strengthen them. You've not only created community and warmed things up, but you've given them a reason to practice *and* a taste of their own capacities, which is confidence building.

Being Real About Suffering

Many of the strategies above make use of two universal methods for creating relevance: discussing the ways we struggle in life, and highlighting the benefits of mindfulness. A common strategy to create buy-in is by defining the problem (e.g., "here's one way we suffer") and then presenting mindfulness training as one component of the solution. Each of us probably can remember being young and feeling mystified that no one was speaking more directly about the suffering that seemed woven into experience. The heart longs for an honest acknowledgement of this dimension of experience.

Being real about the presence of suffering in the lives of young people is a powerful way to build community and establish the relevance of mindfulness.

> **TRY THIS . . .**
> Put yourself (the adult) in the hot seat. It is typical for us as elders to ask kids questions about their life and thoughts. Allow yourself to be the object of inquiry by setting up a structured opportunity (with appropriate boundaries) for your students to ask you questions about your life and experience. Allow them to see you as someone who is human and real.

Speak to the struggles and challenges teens face on a daily basis. Regardless of the context within which you may be working—a school with gang violence, juvenile hall, residential treatment facility, private retreat, or well-resourced charter school—what's universal is that teens and adolescents in our culture are suffering, and too few of the adults around them are being real about that.

In his work with Challenge Day, Collazo meets thousands of young people all over the country. While he notes that there are differences, he points to a common cultural thread that he sees in adolescents:

> Yes, the young kids of color in East Oakland are experiencing a type of trauma that is unique and different than the suffering kids experience in more affluent, private schools. But they're both experiencing violence, depression, loneliness, and a range of difficult situations. Both worlds are lacking the skills, resources and strategies to deal with what's going on in a healthy way. There is deep suffering in our society's youth because there is deep suffering in our adults. There's a dysfunctional relationship to pain in our society. Adults don't know what happiness means or how to process their pain, and so they're passing it down to their kids.

The great gift and potential of working with adolescents is the possibility of cutting through the sense of separateness and isolation. To acknowledge our shared vulnerability fosters a sense of belonging and mutual care. With mindfulness, empathy, and compassion, you can create the conditions for young people to see and understand how connected they are on a deep level. When they open up, share, and really hear one another, healing happens. Charisse Minerva, who also works with teens in a wide range of contexts, affirms Callazo's point: "I have not met a teen of any culture or socio-economic level who does not suffer. That does not exist." She describes an encounter with one young man at a Quaker school in an affluent community, who didn't believe it was fair for him to suffer. He had been holding all of his pain inside, carrying it and feeling ashamed of it all at the same time. In Minerva's mindfulness class, he finally felt safe enough to speak about it. Once he admitted that he was struggling with feeling isolated and depressed, it came out that he wasn't the only one. "It started ricocheting around the group, and it was like they were each taking off this heaviness, just putting down generations of heaviness from holding it all inside."

A feeling of not belonging is another common source of suffering among teens. Bart van Melik speaks of one young person's realization during a group reflection on the use of profanity, "I found out as I'm listening to you all that I do it [use profanity] just to fit in. I've been in three different schools in the last year, and each time I felt like I had to just to fit in." Many young adults also struggle with a harsh inner critic, where self-care or self-compassion may be a foreign concept. Often, the voice inside has become so normalized that they aren't even aware it's an unhealthy habit that can be shifted.

Minerva worked with one young woman who reacted so quickly whenever someone mentioned her mother that she'd have knocked the other kid down to the floor before she even knew what had happened. She was repeatedly expelled and kicked out of schools for her violent outbursts. "I just want to be able to get through school," she complained. Mindfulness practice helped her to begin to see the gap between her emotions and the reaction and to have more choices about how to handle her anger.

Emphasize Choice, Agency, and Personal Goals

Instead of describing what mindfulness is, one of best ways to get kids interested is to discuss the benefits of mindfulness in relation to their goals or challenges. The basic principle is that the more aware you are, the more choice you have. After a short calming meditation, Ervin makes this connection through a game in which two or three kids sit in the center of the room on the "hot seat." Their job is to restrain the impulse to react in any way while the rest of the class is invited to crack jokes and dis them. It's a risky game, requiring clear agreements and intentions, but one that definitely gets the kids energetically engaged! During the debrief, Ervin points out how important the context is: they don't get upset because it's a game, but if it were in the cafeteria they might lose their cool. With a clear intention, they're able to make a decision and control their reaction. He invites them to consider: when you know you're going to be around someone who gets you going, how proactive are you about setting an intention and staying clearly aware of your reactions?

Many educators emphasize the clarity that mindfulness creates internally and the sense of agency and empowerment it confers externally. Dave Smith points out that with mindfulness, "Life isn't just an event that's happening to you; it's not just this random chaos where you hope for the best." Hearing this offers new possibilities for many teens.

Mindfulness puts young people in touch with their innate agency and power. A key part of how this occurs is by changing their relationship to thoughts and emotions. Showing teens that they don't have to believe every thought, that they can choose what to pay attention to, and they can step out of the negative story in their mind is revolutionary. (In fact, this is eye opening for most people new to contemplative practice.) In contrast to the untrained mind that incessantly spins and obsesses, the inner freedom that comes from using the tool of mindfulness to let go of thoughts is remarkable. Minerva describes this revelation: "Mindfulness shows us the walls we've created, the bars of the prison in our own mind. Some kids can hardly believe it when they see this for the first time. 'Are you saying I can take these down?'"

Discuss the value of being aware of different mind states, moods, and emotions. "What would it be like to be able to feel anger without needing to obey what it's telling you to do?" In one lesson, Oren draws a picture of a stick figure within a circle, asking teens, "You know how it feels to be totally consumed by an emotion? It takes over the whole world. What if your awareness were bigger than the emotion?" He then draws another picture with a circle the same size, but the stick figure much larger, so that the circle is now a smaller part of the overall picture. "When mindfulness is strong, we can feel the same emotion but it doesn't overwhelm us. There's more space inside." In the practice, instead of immediately going back to the breath (as one does with concentration practices), give kids guidance to feel and observe their emotions so they learn how to find balance with strong states.

Sometimes our focus on mindfulness techniques obscures the fact that our *view*—how we are looking at things—can impact our level of distress in powerful ways. Mindfulness is not exclusively about present-time awareness; it includes a reappraisal of our life and its challenges. Part of our work is helping adolescents reconceive their lives in more empowering ways. To overlook this is to undervalue the psychoeducational dimensions of mindfulness.

Develop a Repertoire of Strategies

Establishing relevance is not something an educator does once at the beginning of a class. Develop a kind of flexibility and mental literacy that allows you to take a wide range of experiences and comments and tie them back to mindfulness.

An excellent way of doing this is pointing out what's happening in the room in the moment. "I'm really appreciating the level of stillness and quiet in the room. Do you notice that, too?" Call their attention to any aspect of their direct experience that is connected to mindfulness: being present and aware, listening, kindness, trust, courage, and so on. The eminent group psychotherapist, Irvin Yalom emphasizes *here and now* interactions as the engine of therapeutic change. One theory holds that we don't check our interpersonal habits at the door when we enter a therapy room or a school classroom. Instead, the psychological challenges from one's life will manifest within the group context. Exploring what's happening in the *here and now* enlivens the group and highlights important dynamics to which we can bring awareness. In an interview, Yalom (2010) discusses one experience while giving a lecture in China following an earthquake that claimed lives and was traumatizing for the community. He didn't like how the lecture was going:

> I thought we were very distant from each other. I was trying to talk a
> little bit about the here-and-now, but they started off asking me ques-

tions like, "Will you please teach us how to run groups for all these earthquake victims we have?" There were a couple questions like that, and I frankly didn't have a lot to offer them. I haven't done a group for trauma victims before or anything like that. As I was talking about the here-and-now someone popped up . . . "Well, what is the experience for you like here-and-now?" I just love that question.

Yalom responded by sharing that he understood the great needs of the group at this time and was disappointed with his inability to address the depth of suffering being experienced. Acknowledging this truth shifted the mood in the room and the whole talk proceeded differently. Here, Yalom models the way we can shift the emotional ambiance of a group by acknowledging what many might be feeling, but no one is saying.

SOCIAL ENGAGEMENT AND MUTUAL INQUIRY

Creating relevance and building authentic relationships opens the door for young people to share with and learn from each other. As we've already explored, adolescents and young adults are highly focused on peer social relationships. In most respects, they're more interested in speaking to and hearing from each other than with adults. At a time in their lives when social isolation, anxiety, depression, fear, and other painful mental states can be corrosive, having genuine, meaningful conversations with fellow teens and adolescents can be deeply healing (often more so than anything we can say or do as adults). They see firsthand that they are not alone in their suffering. Many teens have a deep hunger for this experience.

In addition to the range of strategies we've already discussed, there are a few ways to create the conditions for these kinds of conversations, both explicitly and implicitly. Implicitly, our own attitude plays a huge role in sparking dialogue among teens. Regard the sessions you lead as a *mutual inquiry*, one in which you're there to learn with and from each other.

There is much we can learn from the young people we serve. Morris Ervin cites an Ethiopian proverb, "To teach is to learn twice." At this age, most young people are still quite open-minded. There is a spaciousness in their thinking that's not fixed. They're pushing boundaries, questioning, and thinking outside of the box in ways that many adults have forgotten. Ask yourself, how open am I to being changed by these young people? You can even invite them to challenge you, with the understanding that you'll learn and grow together from that direct engagement. The more genuinely you are willing to learn and be changed, the more naturally you will create an environment of honesty, openness, and authenticity in which the kids feel comfortable to step forward and share with one another. As Jozen remarked, "I learn more from the youth than I think they learn from me."

How you structure a conversation and engage them in dialogue is another important way to foster interaction and sharing. We can develop an artful use of call and response prompts and questions to establish a rhythmic interaction that implicitly creates safety, trust, and coregulation in the human nervous system.

Neuroscientist Stephen Porges's *The Polyvagal Theory* (2011) proposed a new understanding of the Autonomic Nervous System (ANS). Chris McKenna (2015) summarizes Porges's theory and explores its relevance for teaching mindfulness to adolescents:

> [Porges] took the traditional two-branch understanding of the ANS process—sympathetic (flight and flight) and parasympathetic (rest and digest)—and proposed a further split in the parasympathetic system into two branches—dorsal vagal (DV) and ventral vagal (VV). The DV is the "oldest" part of the ANS (an aspect of functioning that we have in common even with reptiles) and is responsible for what most of us think of as the freeze or immobility response. The VV is the "newest" part of the ANS, bears distinct phylogenetic changes in structure, and is associated with the muscles of the head, neck and inner ear. In

Porges' model, it is responsible for overall social engagement, including the ability to pick up social cues, read micro-expressions, etc. Engaging the ventral vagus system is therefore critical for establishing a sense of safety with others and feeling of being settled in the environment . . . [When this system is "online," the result is an overall internal sense that says] "I can relax here; it's safe to do what I'm doing and engage with this group of people. I feel relaxed yet enlivened when I'm here. I can tell from the teacher's face that they are listening to me, and this gives me the energy to share more."

While the VV can be engaged by using mindfulness to orient to our environment through the senses (instructions like "let your eyes look wherever they want in the room" can be helpful for teens who are easily overwhelmed by thoughts, emotions and internal body sensations), it is easiest to stimulate the VV through well-attuned social engagement. Human beings are social creatures; we're essentially pack animals. As such, one way that we experience interpersonal safety is through a lively "back and forth" exchange of information between members of a group. This call and response is a complex mixture of physiological and vocal interplay. (pp. 2–3)

McKenna goes on to suggest ping-pong as a simple metaphor for this kind of dialogue. Our job is to "send information" to the teens and give them easy opportunities to "send information" back to us. As we do more rounds of this back and forth, a rhythm is established; a sense of flow and engagement mounts, akin to the way good conversations build momentum between friends. This rhythmic engagement signals safety and ease at a deep biological level, along with an attunement to and interest in the immediate environment. This is an ideal state of learning readiness from which to invite young folks to engage in mindfulness practices and explore their experiences with each other.

You can use group facilitation skills to initiate this kind of rhythmic exchange with the class. The general rule here is to engage young folks by turning every piece of didactic content you can into a discussion. This involves flexibly using a range of different kinds of questions in order to meet a group where it's at and slowly get a rhythm going. Many educators enjoy beginning a session by introducing a relevant theme for discussion with an open-ended question. Some common themes might include trust, loyalty, respect, friendship, bullying, or even profanity. "What does loyalty mean to you? Talk about someone who's been loyal." Others will begin by posing a bold, controversial, or interesting question. For example, in a lesson on kindness, an opening question might be, "Are human beings wired to be ethical and compassionate or not?" or "When you think about human history, would you say compassion and ethics are innate and natural or learned?"

In some settings, young folks aren't used to being invited to share their opinions freely and of their own choice. This may show up as a kind of *freeze response* in the room—silence, a deadness or flat energy. When a group feels stuck, in order to shift the energy and get their nervous systems engaged, make it as *easy as possible* for youth to respond. You can draw them out by asking yes/no or polling questions ("How many people think *x*, raise your hand?"). A succession of three to five easy-to-answer polling questions can begin to raise the energy of a group and help to organize their nervous systems.

Ask follow-up and clarifying questions; synthesize their responses and make connections to tie things back to the lesson. Some educators will build the conversation by using a signature refrain question, such as "What do you think?" This can spark discussion while signaling choice and inviting shared ownership of the space. When you employ these strategies wisely to the flow of a class, you see the results. Morris Ervin describes it this way: "You can feel it when they're engaged, you know what that looks like . . . . They're having fun, they're asking questions, smiling, listening to each other."

These are all ways of creating social engagement implicitly. There are many other ways to create that engagement explicitly, from team-building exercises and games to music or dance. Some fun games to break the ice include: Two

Truths and a Lie (sharing two autobiographical facts and one lie and asking others to identify the lie); If You Really Knew Me (self-disclosure activity where students complete the sentence "If you really knew me, you'd know . . ." three different ways); and, Still Chillin' (sitting in a group completely still, and if someone moves—other than breathing and blinking—another student can call out that movement). A curriculum is often just a skeleton to enter into conversation with the kids. As things get going, you can use structured formats for sharing like council practice (using a talking stick in a circle) or working in dyads (designating a speaker and listener) to support safety, trust, and deeper listening.

The true sign that we've been successful in creating genuine engagement and mutual inquiry is that the students begin to learn from and heal with one another. Inviting students to share about their own experiences of being mindful, be it during formal practice, at home, or in the flow of life, gives them the opportunity to validate one another's experience. Bart van Melik shares a story of teaching a class at a residential treatment facility with a group of kids with a high incidence of ADHD and autism spectrum disorder. One student celebrated noticing that he was distracted, and another responded, "Wow, you *noticed* that you were distracted—that's awesome. I was mad distracted but just didn't think I was doing it right."

In these moments, the adolescents begin to embody strength through authentic vulnerability. A quality of empathy and compassion arises that cuts through the illusion of separateness, revealing a felt understanding of how connected they truly are. Hearing one another's inner struggles helps them to realize that they're not alone. ("It's not just me.") Many educators comment on how deeply moving these moments can be, in which teens witness their humanity and join each other in their pain.

Another common insight that emerges from such discussions is the understanding that "hurt people hurt people," and the corresponding realization that if we don't find a way to deal with our own pain in a healthy way, it spills out onto others. This can spark compassion not only for one another, but also for those engaging in harmful activities. One young woman came to Jozen's program at the Brooklyn Zen Center to try to learn tools to express herself differently from the way anger and argument was being modeled at home. He recalls her saying, "I'm here because I want to meet other kids who may be going through what I'm going through. I want to have a conversation and learn from each other how we can work through this. I want to have kids and don't want to pass this on."

The work that we do with young people has the potential for an impact that reaches far beyond our own lifetime. With these practices and these conversations, we can give teens and adolescents the tools to bear witness to their pain and heal the ancient intergenerational wounds.

CHAPTER 6

WORKING WITH RESISTANCE AND OVERCOMING OBSTACLES

After the third or fourth time of asking the young woman to put away her cell phone, the student slowly put the device in her bra and said, "You know what, Bart—come and get it." Bart took a long pause, grounding attention in his body, bringing awareness to his internal experience. Then, with the entire class of 26 students looking at him, he spoke: "I'm just going to say out loud what's happening in me right now. My heart is pounding. I feel quite tense; I'm feeling a lot of heat in my body. I notice that the room is quiet, that I actually have everyone's attention, including yours. I feel a sense of being seen, and that leads to some more calm. And now I'm also starting to feel my breath again, which I'd totally lost. I also notice that we're having eye contact right now, and that we're both paying attention to what's happening in this moment. What I'm teaching, what we're trying to learn about in this class, is happening right now." Having defused the situation and captivated the class's attention, Bart picked up where he'd left off, weaving this new awareness into the lesson. On her way out of the class, the young woman came up to him and said in a friendly way, "You know, Bart, that was all right."

THERE CAN BE MANY OBSTACLES IN TEACHING MINDFULNESS TO ADOLES-cents. In this chapter, we'll delve into some of the challenges that inevitably surface during mindfulness lessons, challenges that any competent teacher must be prepared to address: from behavioral issues with the kids, frequently referred to as *resistance*; to some of our own internal barriers; to more structural challenges in your school or institution.

WORKING WITH RESISTANCE FROM STUDENTS

Responding to behavior issues and encountering resistance are perhaps the most common challenges for educators working with teens and adolescents. When handled with skill, grace, and integrity, these situations can support insight and transformation in a student, deepen connection and relevance, and enhance a group's learning.

Resistance can show up in many different ways, from direct opposition and acting out, to being physically or verbally withdrawn, to a lack of eye contact, and so forth. Some teenagers seem to be able to resist with almost every fiber of their being! Doug Worthen, a high school teacher and mindfulness instructor, puts it this way: "In the first few sessions there can be giggle fits or a sense of skepticism, but week by week they typically become more engaged. Most students just need some time and space to understand what mindfulness actually is and how it is applicable to them" (personal communication).

Jozen Tamori Gibson notes that, "The majority of youth come in with a sense of skepticism, wanting and needing to express themselves as they are and for who they are, but also not quite sure how it's going to be received and if they're going to be held with love and compassion." Sometimes, the level of honesty and vulnerability you offer can be threatening. It can be overwhelming or fear-inducing to be seen or heard, especially when parents or caregivers have been unavailable or abusive. Students may avoid connecting as a way of protecting themselves until they feel safe enough to open up; they actually may be taking in your care whether they show it or not.

Resistance also can be an indication that you've moved too quickly into the meditation, that you haven't established enough relevance, or that your lesson's topic isn't attuned to them. If you're not meeting the kids where they are, they may resist or act out to let you know that they're not feeling connected to what you're inviting them to do. For example, if you come in following a curriculum plan on kindness and there was just a big fight, the students may have great difficulty finding meaning in the ideas.

There are a range of strategies and perspectives to working with such challenging behaviors. These can be summarized in three basic levels or dimensions of response. The first two form the internal basis of the response, while the third encompasses the range of responses that flow from that internal basis.

1. **Check your assumptions.** Align your understanding of the situation with a perspective that is conducive to connection and transformation.
2. **Handle your internal state.** Rely on your own personal practice to process any reactivity so that you can come from a place of inner composure and choice.
3. **Engage the resistance.** Employ various relational strategies, basic communication techniques, and counseling tools to meet the situation skillfully.

Check Your Assumptions

One of the greatest challenges to effectively working with resistance is to avoid viewing the behaviors we call *resistance* as a something negative. In psychology, the concept of resistance describes a client's direct or indirect opposition to changing behaviors, discussing experiences, or assenting to a clinician's intervention. However, viewing of students' actions as resistance can inhibit your ability to connect with them, block access to positive intentions, and exacerbate your own internal distress or reactivity.

Instead, see if you can view such behaviors as valuable information about a young person's needs, drawing a distinction between their actions and what's inside, driving those actions. These behaviors are entirely normal for adolescents and are often a part of their process of psychological differentiation and identity formation. The behavior might be an attempt to communicate the student's inner experience, to self-regulate, or to exercise autonomy. This shift in your own thinking can help you to stay connected to intentions of curiosity and care and create new possibilities for engaging.

Psychologist and founder of the Center for Adolescent Studies, Sam Himelstein (2013), urges educators not to pathologize behaviors as resistance, but to see them as powerful doorways to insight for clients:

> [Such behaviors] serve a specific purpose: they protect the ego against negative states of being and, in extreme situations, from trauma. When exploring the present moment with a client and looking for what type of resistance or mechanism is manifesting, there is the potential for the client to become aware of such mechanisms, gain insight into their origin, and learn and practice taking action with them. A person who has the ability to become aware of his or her primary protective mechanisms and resistance patterns and to choose whether or not to employ them has the ability to transcend what is commonly thought of as a part of personality. This response is associated with great insight and awareness. (p.137)

At the heart of this shift in perspective lies the ability to access empathy for the kids. Collazo describes his own experience of empathy when leading a Challenge Day: "In the moment, as I'm looking out into that sea of young eyes, I start tearing up because I know there is someone in that crowd who's

getting beat up, or thinking about killing themselves, or living with someone who's addicted. In a room of 100 kids, you just look at the percentages
and you know what's happening." Keeping this perspective in mind allows
him to see their posturing or other challenging behaviors as self-protection, as
defense mechanisms that serve some important needs for them.

To do this requires checking your assumptions. Be wary of thoughts
that say you know what is happening for a student or that attribute mali-
cious intentions to their behavior. We really can't know what's going on for
them. Give them the benefit of the doubt. Behavior issues can arise due to any
number of conditions—from stress at home to unmet physiological needs for
food or sleep. Tish Jennings (2018) suggest a similar shift from the question,
"What's wrong with him?" to "What happened to him and how did he learn
to adapt to it?" (p. 50).

Sometimes, what we call resistance can simply be due to excess energy.
(Recognizing this, many educators choose to begin their sessions with some
movement to help modulate and settle any strong energy in their students.)
Often, resistance can be part of teens' way of checking you out. In order to
gauge whether or not they'll be able to relate to you, young folks will watch
you carefully, observing how you engage, how you relate to others, and in particular *how you handle behavior issues*. They're waiting for you to mess up or to
give some sign of who you really are when under pressure. They want to know
if they can trust you, how you respond to a class that's out of control. Are you
going to freak out or stay engaged?

Handle Your Internal State

Shifting our perspective is the first step to opening the door to transformation. The next step is our ability to tolerate and successfully manage any reactivity that arises in relation to students' behavior. As educators, we care deeply
about our work with young people. It can be incredibly frustrating when one
or more students seem to be doing everything they can to undermine your
intentions or inhibit learning in the classroom. Your ability to respond effec-

tively to such behavior issues is directly proportional to your capacity to manage internal reactivity. Raising your voice or losing your cool can damage the relationships you've worked so hard to build.

Here, your own personal practice is your greatest ally. The combination of nonreactive awareness, inner stability, spaciousness, and flexibility one develops in formal mindfulness practice is an asset when facing stressful moments in the classroom. The more deeply you have contemplated and learned to hold with care your human emotions of frustration, anger, fear, anxiety, or helplessness in meditation, the more deftly you will be able to manage those waves in the moment with students. In reflecting on the incident with a student putting her cell phone in her bra, van Melik (2018) attributes his skillful response to his own practice: "That only happened, I think, because there was some room in my mind to be still creative in the midst of my buttons being so pushed" (p. 88).

Mindfully track your inner experience—thoughts, emotions and sensations—and find balance in the moment. Use the tools of mindfulness practice to recognize your internal state, ground your attention in your body, and create enough space to allow the intensity of your present moment experience to subside enough to respond instead of reacting automatically. Here are a few ways of consciously using your attention to create more internal space and handle strong emotions in response to challenging behaviors:

+ Take one or more mindful breaths.
+ Do a very brief body scan.
+ Feel your feet on the floor or the sensations in the palms of your hands.
+ Ground your attention by relaxing your upper body and bending the knees slightly, increasing sensations of pressure and heaviness in your feet.
+ Briefly observe the thoughts, sensations, and emotions that are occurring, labeling them mentally to create some inner space or perspective.
+ Widen your awareness to hearing sounds.

+ Attune to the visual space in the room.
+ Pause using gesture, facial expression, or subvocal expression (e.g., "*Hmmm*").
+ Commit internally to being nondefensive.
+ Make a short statement indicating that you are taking time. *"I'm taking a moment to decide how I'd like to respond."*

If you notice yourself getting regularly activated by one student in particular, take time outside of class to investigate your feelings and triggers. What's actually happening? Where are you getting hooked? Are you taking a student's behavior personally? The more we take a situation personally, feeling threatened, judging ourselves, or seeking approval, the less likely we are to respond in an appropriate, creative, or skillful way. Remember that there are many factors in a student's life that have nothing to do with you!

Be mindful of the tendency to judge yourself, avoid uncomfortable emotions, or shut down intense feelings. Instead, make space to experience the full range of your emotions: frustration, anger, disappointment, sadness, helplessness, insecurity. Imagine the worst-case scenario to face your fears. Once you acknowledge that, it has less power. Again, the more you work through your feelings outside of class, the easier it will be to stay clear, grounded, and calm in class.

Engage the Resistance

Aligning our perspective with a view that is conducive to connection (seeing these behaviors as powerful protective mechanisms rather than pathology) and learning to handle our own reactivity forms the foundation of a skillful response to student behavior issues. From this base of clear seeing and internal presence, we are able to wisely employ a range of interventions and strategies to meet what's happening in the moment.

To engage the resistance means to meet the energy in a person or in the room and work with it creatively. The basic formula is to first acknowledge what's happening, then invite dialogue and mutual exploration, and last create an agreement or plan for moving forward.

First acknowledge what's happening. Describe the behavior or situation calmly, in a neutral, specific, and nonblaming way, which reduces the chances that the student will hear your response as an attack or immediately classify it as another attempt to control their behavior. Naming what's happening also calls the student and the group into a shared experience of present-moment awareness.

Then, invite the student into a process of mutual exploration about the actual situation, statement, behavior, or event in question. Rather than imposing your own interpretation or demanding a specific course of action, use whatever is occurring as an opportunity to apply the tools of mindful investigation together. Himelstein (2018) suggests using reflective statements and questions to name and explore. These invite the other person, "to reflect on themselves in some way, to potentially gain insight into what's happening for them in that moment." The reflective nature of the engagement opens the door to learning and self-awareness.

This approach is distinct from more traditional, directive behavior-modification interventions that maintain standard power dynamics. It relies on your ability to access empathy and prioritize the quality of connection in the relationship over any particular outcome. You're not imposing your power; nor are you relinquishing your power. Ultimately you can't make anyone do anything, but *how* you engage can communicate volumes more than *what* you say. Becoming fixated on behavior modification or changing the student's mind creates the perfect conditions for a power struggle. What's more, a punitive approach will only reinforce the sense of separation, isolation, or shame that we are trying to heal through this work.

Here are a few examples of how you might use this two-step process of acknowledging what's happening and inviting dialogue. Notice how these differ from the first response, which illustrates a more directive approach that maintains standard power dynamics.

> **Rather than:** *"You're acting out a lot today. Do you need to step outside and a break?"*
> **Try:** *"It seems like you've got a lot of energy today, huh? I'm curious what's going on. How are you doing?"*

> **Rather than:** *"You're being disrespectful. Do you want to rephrase that?"*
> **Try:** *"I'm guessing you feel pretty strongly about what you just said, is that right? I want to honor the intensity of what you're feeling, and I also want to honor our agreement about mutual respect. Would you be up for sharing about more about how you're feeling?"*

> **Rather than:** *"Will you please pick your head up and pay attention?"*
> **Try:** *"I notice you've had your head down most of the time I've been here today, and I'm just wondering where you're at?"*

These reflective statements and questions are intended to open a dialogue. As you engage, seek a way to meet their underlying needs, win a student over, redirect the energy, or (if all else fails) contain the behavior. Explore what's happening for the student. Make space to show empathy and offer understanding for their feelings to de-escalate any tension. Then, seek to under-stand their concerns and needs. Ask questions and really listen to what they say. Inquire, directly or indirectly, what matters for them. "What do you need right now?" can be a powerful question.

After you identify what's going on, brainstorm ways they can meet their needs that also honor the needs of other students in the room. Communicate clearly your desire to balance your care for them with your need to support everyone's learning. Brainstorming together in this way models mutual respect and sharing power, which can build the relationship.

If you're unable to find a strategy that works for both of you, suggest alternatives that honor the student's autonomy while still supporting the rest of the group's desire to learn. "It's totally fine for me if you find this boring or if you're not interested in trying this practice. What I'm asking is if you can hang out and sit quietly, without making noise or distracting others, while the rest of us give it a go. Is it okay with you if we do this?"

Throughout this process, tone is everything. Relate to the behavior as you would relate to a difficult mind state, thought, or emotion in your own mindfulness practice: bring as much compassion, patience, and curiosity to bear as you can. Do your best to speak and relate in a way that is calm, clear, and kind, modeling respect and a nondemanding, collaborative approach. This helps to build the relationship and honors adolescents' need for autonomy. Give particular emphasis to maintaining a sense of congruence between your internal experience and your external behavior. As we've seen, adolescents are hyper-attuned to incongruence. If your internal experience and your external behavior don't match, this can actively work against your ability to build the relationship and creatively redirect energy.

To engage the resistance, it's also important to be willing to let go of the plan. The more tightly you hold to your lesson plan, the less flexibility you will experience to respond creatively to what's happening in the moment with the students. Do your best to let go of expectations about how mindfulness *should* go and focus on responding authentically to whatever comes up as you teach.

Can you trust your capacity to be with this young person, connect, and allow wisdom to guide your response? If you are able to hold those plans lightly, you may find yourself opening a rich conversation with the students about a theme connected to what's actually alive in the room.

Another way to engage the resistance is to point out the strengths and good qualities in the person who is acting out. See how much the person has to offer. If someone is constantly co-opting the attention and taking over the class, instead of focusing on the negative side, consider their leadership potential. Give them a task or some responsibility in the group. It may take time and patience to help them to discover and own their strengths and how to express their gifts in constructive ways.

Khalila Gillett Archer recounts the story of one young man who attended a few teen retreats with iBme and had been diagnosed with oppositional defiant disorder. He'd been labeled a troublemaker and anti-authority. His behavior was consistent: he'd push back against anything an adult said. Instead of engaging in a power struggle, the staff showed him the respect they were inviting him to exhibit by doing their best to give him space, while lovingly setting firm, clear boundaries. Over time, things started to shift. He softened on his own. He'd come back for another retreat and hug the staff, showing much love and respect.

Archer comments, "It didn't feel like that much work to get there. Some people have this belief that you really need to get out the chisel and dig to deal with resistance. Often, their hearts are right there under the surface, just waiting for us to create a little bit of space and understanding. Those protective mechanisms are there for a reason. If we push against them, they usually push back. We don't come in with some agenda that they need to change, and that's part of what allows them to relax and open up."

Reset the Parameters

Timing is another factor in working with resistance. Choose which interventions to use in class, and when to find a neutral time to talk privately with the student(s) in question. Some instructors prefer to build into their program time to meet with students one on one or in pairs, so that kids have a space to get individualized attention instead of needing to act out in class.

Using group agreements is another indispensable tool for working with behavior issues (see Chapter 4). These agreements provide a simple structure for behavior etiquette that helps students to know what you expect of them and why. If things get rocky, you can refer back to the agreements and the intentions behind them, enlisting the support of other students. This is a delicate process in which educators must take care to use their authority skillfully, setting an appropriate boundary while maintaining the relationship of trust and mutual respect. For example, Himelstein (2013) includes a group agreement about refocusing in all of his classes. If kids start talking over each other or lose focus, he'll pause mindfully, check his own intentions, and then quietly and calmly repeat a short request like, "Hey fellas, can we all please be quiet for a few moments?" (p. 122). Students begin to pause and often help remind each other to do so. It doesn't take long before he has the group's undivided attention.

Another approach is to invite the class to have an honest conversation about their intentions for learning and how we get along with one another. What do the other students need to be able to learn? Do they have ideas about how to work together to address the situation? Belonging is such a deep need for teens and adolescents that if you've laid the proper groundwork, the students will begin reminding one another of the group agreements and guide each other back to the group norms. If this is not happening organically, speak privately with one or two students who are leaders in the class and invite their input. Encourage them to speak up or help set behavior norms.

Ideally, you've created a meaningful and supportive learning environment and set a clear and strong container from the beginning. If not, it can be difficult to go back and redefine the ground rules. However, with some care, skill, and planning, it can be done. If appropriate, consider doing a *reset* with your class: discuss everyone's needs; reaffirm group agreements and norms; and work to reestablish a culture of respect.

Setting clear limits from the beginning is important to establish trust, safety, and respect. It's essential to use your discernment about where to draw the line, so that it's grounded in something authentic and concrete—such as the group agreements or your desire to create an environment in which everyone can learn—rather than more arbitrary notions of behavioral norms. Know the difference in yourself between playful social connection and disruptive or harmful behavior. When a student does cross that line, be willing to address it directly and immediately so that there's clarity about your expectations. Being kind is different from being nice. We can say "no" with a heart of compassion and care. Even though we associate kindness with "yes," adolescents cannot trust us when we say "yes" unless they also know we're empowered to say "no."

How we set that limit is extremely important for teens and adolescents, who are in a developmental process of renegotiating their relationship to power by questioning authority and asserting their autonomy. In the role of mentor, educators must balance their friendship with teens together with a willingness to step into authority and create healthy structure. When you need to set a limit, be fiercely compassionate, without judgment or blame. Make your requests clear, specific, and doable, and share the reasons behind what you are asking them to do. This inherently acknowledges their autonomy and helps create buy-in. If and when you need to use your power to enforce limits (e.g., asking a student to leave), be sure to frame it in terms of your values or goals (e.g., wanting everyone to learn) rather than "right" and "wrong," which can undercut a student's sense of self-worth. Afterwards, it can be helpful to circle back and reconnect with the young person to close the loop. Affirm your care for them. Let them know that you see them, that you're not trying to call them out, and that you're not holding anything against them or maintaining a grudge.

YOUR OWN PERSONAL BARRIERS

In addition to the challenges we encounter from adolescents directly, we may find ourselves hitting personal barriers in our teaching. We've already mentioned several of these potential pitfalls: making assumptions about what's going on for a student, trying to control the situation, holding too tightly to our role or authority, feeling triggered, having difficulty handling our own emotions, and burnout.

Beyond these stumbling blocks, another set of common barriers you may encounter working with teens and adolescents is, ironically enough, your own unresolved adolescent issues. Matthew remembers teaching a group of teens who had arrived at an off-site location. One of the adolescents showed up late and Matthew was escorting him to the welcoming area where a group of 25 teens were playing get-to-know-you type interactive exercises and games. Matthew asked the young man how he was feeling. "Nervous to be going to meet the group." In that moment, Matthew realized the teen was speaking for both of them. Even though he was the senior teacher and a supposed authority figure, Matthew felt exactly like a middle-school kid about to walk into a school dance. Would he be accepted?

Working with teens will bring you face to face with any unresolved psychological issues from your own adolescence. The fear of being excluded, the desire to be liked, and any awkwardness or social uncertainty will rise to the surface. Depending on how you relate to these impulses, they will either direct your behavior or lead to self-understanding and increased inner stability. Educator and youth mentor Morris Ervin talks about the moment he recognized that there was a 16-year-old inside who still wanted to be accepted and was trying to impress the kids. In his desire to please, he gave one of his students a ride home and was hanging out in a rough part of town. It was about dusk and the student said, "Mr. Ervin, it's about time for you to leave—it's going to get unsafe here." In that moment, Morris realized that he had lost his wider awareness of the context and a younger part of himself had been in the driver's seat.

Be prepared for these challenges to arise internally. What part of you wants to fit in and be accepted? Is there a part that instinctively rebels against authority figures? Do you find yourself longing to have fun with your students as a way to avoid more difficult conversations? Doing one's own psychological healing (particularly around family of origin and teen years) prior to or alongside your work with young people reduces the chances that you'll act out old patterns. You don't need to have resolved every emotional issue in your life, but you must have the capacity to be aware of your own psychological material. When past wounds or challenges do get activated, bring mindfulness to bear on those emotions, memories, and impulses. Meet these areas with care, sensitivity, and a willingness to be vulnerable in order to keep them from taking over or interfering with your work.

Connected to these psychological patterns is the danger of unconsciously putting your own needs first, which complicates the relationship. Working with young adults can be incredibly rewarding. The admiration, care, and closeness that can arise in working with kids are remarkable. As Jessica Morey, executive director of iBme notes, "When teens open up, they'll really love you." While there is plenty of nourishment and meaning in the work, be brutally honest with yourself about your intention. It's essential to keep one's primary focus on serving and supporting the adolescents, rather than doing the work in order to fulfill personal needs for connection, belonging, or love. Make sure you are finding other areas of your adult life to meet your needs for recognition, appreciation, belonging, and love. If your own needs begin to take center stage, it can interfere in important ways with building trust and teaching. For example, if your desire for approval or belonging supersedes your interest in their learning or well-being, it can be hard to set limits or enforce agreements.

Sustain Yourself

As we've already explored, it's essential to maintain a solid support network of peers and engage in self-care practices. If you're exhausted, depleted, or burned out, you can't be effective. While you may be the only person standing up in front of the classroom, you're not alone. Turn to friends and colleagues for support. Seek consultation from peers or mentors. Lack of self-care and isolation make it even more challenging (if not impossible) to effectively handle behavior challenges. Be proactive about asking for help from other adults (e.g., an aide, a student teacher) to implement any strategies you choose. Try obtaining one-on-one support for the student, which can be very effective in addressing behavior issues.

If you find yourself venting about a particular student to a colleague or loved one, try to tune into the release that you might feel. Allow yourself to receive the support and comfort of a listening ear. However, don't be totally convinced by the rant—seek to understand the holes in your own logic; rants always leave something out. The more deeply we look into a situation, the more likely we are to find some measure of compassion for both ourselves and the others involved.

Another pervasive personal barrier in working with adolescents is the belief that you have to save, rescue, or fix them. This can lead to unhealthy boundaries or narrow your attention to one or two students. What's more, it creates an imbalanced relationship to the work and your emotional connection to your students, which can lead to frustration, helplessness, and burnout. It takes a certain kind of inner balance and wisdom to recognize the limits of our control in this work. There is a lot of good that we can do, yet there are so many factors in any person's life that it is beyond our capacity to determine the outcome of our teaching with anyone, let alone completely protect or *save* individuals. Coming to terms with this reality can be heartbreaking. If we are to sustain our energy in this work, it's essential to trust that we are planting seeds in each student, seeds that will have a life of their own and will grow in their own time.

STRUCTURAL AND INSTITUTIONAL BARRIERS

So far in this chapter we have explored a range of strategies for working with resistance in our students, as well as given a brief overview of some of the personal barriers we may encounter in this work. We may also face a wide range of structural barriers. These can range from a general lack of institutional support to a hostile faculty member or administrator or from scheduling and space limitations, to poor funding, to community members set on shutting down your program. These conditions point to the reality that we require a certain measure of institutional and community support to share our skills as teachers and facilitators with adolescents.

While we wish to focus primarily on the personal tools and perspectives you will need to share mindfulness with adolescents, we would be remiss in not acknowledging the importance of the setting and context of your program. There is an art to building a robust network and educating a school community about mindfulness so that your program has adequate support. Here are a few tips to keep in mind when introducing, creating, and running a mindfulness program:

+ Prioritize building relationships in the school, agency, institution, and surrounding community. Even one dedicated ally can be worth hours of your time.
+ Emphasize the secular nature of mindfulness and be prepared to answer questions about its relationship to religious freedom.
+ When engaging with stakeholders and community members, listen first. Aim to understand their needs and concerns, and try to address them in a responsive way rather than simply touting the benefits of mindfulness.
+ Be realistic about the benefits and limitations of mindfulness; don't overpromise.
+ Advocate for the value and relevance of mindfulness, being gentle but firm in your persistence.

- If serving as an outside provider, communicate your needs clearly and directly to administrators and staff prior to your program. Aim for regularly scheduled meetings to discuss how the program is going for everyone involved.
- Make clear agreements about what the school or institution can provide and when.
- Make clear requests and agreements with other adults present about how they can support the program.
- See the Further Resources section for information about groups and organizations offering training in starting a mindfulness program.

In terms of connecting with young people, creating relevance and handling resistance, the *setting* of a program can present its own challenges. In contexts where teens are required to attend your class (e.g., juvenile hall, certain schools, residential treatment facilities), it's essential to acknowledge their need for autonomy and find a way to create buy-in. When *external* choice and power are limited by circumstance, highlight the potential benefits of *internal* choice and power that can generate interest in mindfulness. Pay particular attention to your use of language, subtly reinforcing their ability to choose how they participate (as we discussed in Chapter 5). Naming that it's mandatory and thanking them nonetheless for being there also can be a step in the right direction. When adults make mindfulness programs required for teens (often as an intervention for stress, anxiety, or behavior management), the young people usually want to know if the staff is going to participate. Getting participation from the other adults is another way to create buy-in from the teens.

CONSIDER THIS . . .

Offer the staff of your school or institution a weekly meditation class. Share with them in real time what you are doing with the students. Give them the same practices, games, assignments. The kids love hearing that their teachers or administrators are having the same experiences that they are. When JoAnna teaches at institutions, she makes it a requirement for the staff members to come to at least one class.

Many adults working in compulsory public education or other agencies find the predominance of top-down hierarchical approaches challenging and have difficulty thriving in such institutional cultures. Here it's essential to stay clear about one's values, modeling the change we wish to see as consistently as possible. Finding community with like-minded educators outside the setting is an essential support for these challenges.

Another important way to create buy-in and address structural challenges in institutional settings is to work with the staff first. In many contexts, there are one or two champions of mindfulness with little support from the rest of the community. In others, there can be a *fix it* mentality with the expectation that mindfulness will solve all of the problems. It may not occur to the staff—be they clinicians, teachers, correctional officers, or residential counselors—that they too could benefit from the training! Meet with the adults present to establish a shared understanding of your program, its aims and goals as well as its limits. Try to instill the value that "it takes a village to raise a child." The most successful programs for youth involve not just one or two adults but a supportive community surrounding the kids. Engage those who are interested, and try to get agreement from the rest to silently support the program (or at least to not interfere), articulating the specific support that you need from the other adults to make the program a success. Hold out the possibility for real change, while being clear that mindfulness is not a panacea.

CHAPTER 7

ANGER, SELF-HARSHNESS, AND SELF-COMPASSION

One mindfulness teacher recounts a story of teaching a class on self-care in juvenile hall. One girl, 14 years old, said, "I don't deserve self-care and I really don't deserve compassion for myself. You probably can't even give me one example, because I really did something horrible and I don't deserve it." The instructor felt the pressure of being put on the spot; then he had an idea. The kids were often complaining about the temperature in juvenile hall. In the winter it'd be quite hot on the unit; in the summer it was very cold. "Do you ever wake up sometimes and notice your arm is really cold? What do you usually do? Do you change your position or cover your arm?" She did. "Would you consider that an act of compassion? You suffer, and do something about it." She agreed, everyone kind of nodded and pondered the implications.

THINK BACK ON YOUR OWN ADOLESCENT YEARS. With the dramatic physical and psychological changes, we experience a range of intense emotions. Our ability to guide the adolescents in our care toward more balance and self-understanding depends in part on our own familiarity with our inner life. In this chapter, we'll describe how to engage one especially prominent emotion—anger—in ourselves and explore the ways that we support adolescents to navigate anger effectively. We'll also look into the ways that anger can be directed inwards in the form of self-harshness and how self-compassion can be a healing antidote to this tendency.

As we've discussed, adolescence is animated by the hunger for autonomy. Along with the yearning for independence, many teens and young adults experience varying degrees of anger and what could be called antiestablishment attitudes. There are many ways we might understand the prevalence of anger among adolescents. Some of this anger may be an expression of a healthy individuation process. Anger often serves to sharpen the contours of differentiation between self and family or self and culture. Although adolescents are sometimes caricatured as self-involved, they are often mobilized by social justice concerns beyond the narrow purview of their own lives. Anger can be the alarm bell signaling injustice and catalyzing action. In our view, these are healthy causes of anger.

Yet we cannot assume that our own experience of anger mirrors the experience of anger in another. While some features of our emotional lives are universal, much is particular to our own history and conditioning. The way emotion forms and expresses itself is idiosyncratic, an autobiographical experience. Anger arises in the face of threat or obstacles, conditions that haven't been distributed equally across the population. Adolescents from marginalized groups are likely to have experienced disproportionate challenges, and this frequently impacts their history and relationship with anger. Martha Nussbaum (2003), a noted philosopher, said that we must understand an emotion within the larger context of its narrative history. Emotions are part of a larger story about threat and opportunity, danger and safety. If we are to meet the emotional lives of adolescents with genuine, accurate empathy, we must stay attuned to the realities of their history.

Adolescents sometimes feel out of control in their anger and may genuinely seek support for navigating its intensity. As adults, if we are to offer such support, we must learn to tolerate their anger without becoming entangled in it, even when it might be directed at us. This entails developing a more nuanced relationship with anger—our own and the anger of others. Unless we have had conscious experiences of our own anger and learned to work with it skillfully, the effectiveness of our support for adolescents will be limited. We cannot be afraid of their anger or allow their anger to close our heart. When adolescents understand that we can weather the storms of their feelings without becoming defensive or withdrawing our care, their trust and safety in us deepens. Perhaps more importantly, they sense that they too might be able to withstand the intensity of their own emotions without being overwhelmed or defined by them.

More than other emotions, anger often elicits strong moralistic views. We may judge ourselves for experiencing anger in the first place. Or we see anger in our students or colleagues and judge them. Because unchecked anger can cause so much harm in our lives and the world, we assume that the emotion itself also must be harmful. It is possible to stand firmly against the harmful acts that can arise from anger, without judging or rejecting the actual experience of the emotion. What would it be like to be fully committed to not harming others, while at the same time being fully willing to experience anger in a nonjudgmental way? This is the investigation into handling anger and healing our own pain. We don't need to take our emotions personally, reflexively evaluating ourselves as if our emotions were a commentary on the deepest parts of ourselves. Instead, we can take an open and curious stance, honoring the reality of a feeling, at the same time as we try to grow toward more peace and emotional balance.

ESTABLISHING MOTIVATION FOR WORKING WITH ANGER

The state of anger is gripping. Emotional sensations (feelings) tangle with thoughts, creating a state of inner pressure that makes it feel urgent to say or do something. As we will see, there can be wisdom contained within anger, which can be distilled from the distortions of hatred and aggression. Due in part to this intensity, it takes energy to work skillfully with anger. The path of least resistance is whatever habit has been strongest—and often our habits around anger are not skillful. To transform an unskillful habit, we need to marshal our effort effectively. As we begin to approach anger, substantial motivation is required to withstand the rigors of that emotional terrain.

There are many ways to develop and deepen our motivation to explore anger. We can reflect on the fact that how we tend to our own anger will impact how we tend to the anger of students, colleagues, friends, or family. Take some time to consider the kinds of relationships you want to develop in your life or the ways in which you would like to support others. Recognize that the more skill and familiarity you have with your own anger, the more flexibility and freedom you will have when others are angry. These reflections can provide potent fuel for facing the discomfort of our own anger.

Another way to develop motivation for working with anger is to reflect on the harm that has been caused due to unchecked aggression. We have each been harmed by the anger of others, and we have each harmed others through our own anger. Sometimes, it's the closest relationships—parents, children, and partners—where anger seems to arise most intensely. From the interpersonal to the international stage, the effects of this emotion, when not met with awareness, are apparent. Some of the most painful chapters in human history are the story of hatred. Without simplifying complex historical events, we can note that antipathy and hatred are often one of the factors in the perpetration of harm and violence. His Holiness the Dalai Lama (2009) said, "Generally speaking, there are many different kinds of afflictive emotions . . . .But out of all these, hatred and anger are considered to be the greatest [dangers] because they are the greatest obstacles to developing compassion and altruism." Recognizing the potentially harmful effects of unconsciously acting out our anger, we can find great energy to work with anger for the benefit of ourselves *and* others.

The Sheep in Wolf's Clothing

You've probably heard the saying, "a wolf in sheep's clothing." What is truly harmful sometimes comes dressed up looking harmless. Our feelings—especially anger—are more like *sheep dressed as wolves*. Our emotions appear big and imposing; they're designed to get us to make snap judgments and act. At times, they feel so urgent they scare us into action. It seems as if unless we do something, they'll tear us apart. But what are these feelings in and of themselves? Are they more like a wolf or a sheep? What would happen if we did nothing but let them rattle around our mind and course through our body? Remembering and appreciating the sheep-like nature of feelings can help us develop skill with our own anger and support adolescents to navigate the same terrain.

We each have our own particular tendencies with anger. We may express anger in many different ways, often falling along a spectrum from the explosive to the implosive. At one end of the spectrum, there is a clinical diagnosis known as intermittent explosive disorder, which is characterized by abrupt and intense episodes of verbal or physical aggression that are grossly disproportionate to the external stimulus. This affects a surprisingly large proportion of the population: approximately 4% of the population have had this disorder at some point in the past year. If intermittent explosive disorder represents one end of the spectrum, total avoidance and suppression is the other end of the spectrum. Sometimes anger feels so dangerous or destabilizing that people do absolutely everything they can in order to avoid feeling anger and any conflicts that might elicit it. Compulsively avoiding all forms of conflict distorts our behavior and constrains our life.

Between these two ends of the spectrum, there lie many different expressions and experiences of anger. We can consider, what is my relationship to anger? *Progress is going to look different for each of us.* Progress for the person with a more explosive anger style might be to learn how to de-escalate emotion, soothe oneself, make wise decisions in the moment, and forgive others. For the strongly conflict-avoidant person, progress might involve tolerating the experience of anger more fully and finding assertive ways of expressing one's feelings and needs. Skillfully expressing our anger can be a very important aspect of emotional health. As one of the characters in Shakespeare's *The Taming of the Shrew* says, "My tongue will tell the anger of my heart, Or else my heart concealing it will break." Sometimes, anger can only be resolved through sharing our experience.

Being with intense emotions can feel a little bit like getting into a pool of cold water. At first we may squirm and scream, taking quick, shallow breaths and longing to get out. But if the water isn't too cold, our body adjusts and we can actually get used to it. We find some ease with what previously felt almost intolerable. In the same way, when we learn to swim in our emotions—including anger—what felt intolerable can become much more manageable. We can bear it. Of course this takes practice, for ourselves and our students. One aspect of our formal meditation is practicing sitting in water that is sometimes too cold.

The Vietnamese meditation teacher, author, and activist Thich Nhat Hanh (nominated for the Nobel Peace Prize by Martin Luther King Jr.) offers another metaphor for learning to feel our anger. A central image in his book *Anger: Wisdom for Cooling the Flames* (2002) is caring for our anger as one might care for a child. He writes, "Just like our organs, our anger is part of us. When we are angry, we have to go back to ourselves and take good care of our anger. We cannot say, 'Go away, anger, I don't want you.' When you have a stomachache, you don't say, 'I don't want you stomach, go away.' No, you take care of it. In the same way, we have to embrace and take good care of our anger" (p. 56). This is a powerful attitude for approaching anger. Rather than demonizing the experience or demonizing ourselves, we actually turn toward our experience with kindness, care, and a commitment not to create additional suffering for ourselves or others.

This ability to meet anger and other emotions with kind awareness is supported by a particular perspective at the heart of mindfulness practice. Mindfulness is both a technique and a way of *viewing* experience. It suggests that we view emotion as a natural, innocent expression of our own evolutionary history. Emotions evolved to serve us, and even when an emotion might be maladaptive in a particular situation, we can remember that our body and mind are simply running the software we inherited. From this perspective, it's okay to feel any and all emotions. Mindfulness teaches us to know emotional experience as a product of nature, like the wind and weather. In this way, we're establishing a view of our mental and emotional life that is conducive to emotional balance.

Radical Accountability Without Self-Blame

There are two complementary attitudes that support our ability to work with anger skillfully (or any emotion, for that matter). Without both, our approach to anger can become unbalanced. We'll call these attitudes *radical accountability* and the *blamelessness of feeling*. Radical accountability means that we take responsibility for the experience of anger. When we get angry, the mind always becomes focused on the *object* of our anger. It appears as if the person or the experience created our anger. Part of what we're learning in mindfulness practice is that the seeds of anger lie within; the targets of our frustration stimulate those seeds, rather than plant them. Radical accountability doesn't mean we ignore the behavior that may have elicited the anger, but we refuse to fully externalize the cause of the anger. We refuse to point at someone or something and end the inquiry there. Mindfulness practice helps us look more deeply at our minds in that moment and be honest about patterns that we observe in our lives. We may recognize that anger is a habit we've nourished over years. We detect the triggers for our anger. While we can acknowledge that there are external sparks for our anger, that spark is insufficient for the fire of anger to erupt. We contribute, too. This humbling recognition helps us take responsibility for our experience of anger.

The blamelessness of feeling is a complementary attitude that supports the commitment to radical accountability. While we take responsibility to care for our anger, we can know that anger is not manufactured solely by the ego. We often assume that somewhere inside us is an engine from which all of our feelings emerge. That engine feels like the essence of our being. But this way of construing our emotions leads us to take our inner life too personally. Anger and all feelings arise out of a million influences and conditions outside of ourselves. Even as our thoughts, interpretations, and responses play a role in *fueling* anger, we are not the one generating the emotion of anger; it is a universal response across all different species. Anger occurs because many other conditions have fallen into place. It is not a decision. We didn't design our nervous system or our evolutionary history. We didn't design the events of the day, of the week, of our life. Anger is not our fault. We can relax into that innocence. Staying in contact with this insight about our innocence helps us take good care of our anger.

This understanding is also a powerful lens through which to see the anger of our students and colleagues. Just as we personalize our own anger, the anger of our students is often interpreted in highly personal ways. If a student directs anger at us, it is tempting to construe it as an attack on our own being. That interpretation, however, is unlikely to prompt a skillful response from us and may create a downward spiral of mutual resentment. Instead, we can see that their anger emerges out of many forces and is in fact not a commentary on who we are. We can understand their anger as an expression of an unmet need. This empowers us to navigate the fire of anger without fearing that we'll get burned.

Anger, Discernment, and Delusion

Sometimes anger can contain real clarity and provide wisdom about a situation. When we are able to tolerate the rush of feeling that comes with anger and distill its meaning from the storm of the emotion, it can inform our course of action in a skillful way. Perhaps the anger helps us recognize that someone is taking advantage of another person. Perhaps anger helps us recognize injustice and motivates us to act.

While there may be occasional clarity in our anger, we suggest that there is always a seed of delusion also present in anger. *The story our anger tells us is never the last word.* If we look more deeply at the complexity of the situation, details will emerge that we were not seeing in the moment of anger. When we more fully understand the person who may be triggering the anger, the story must change. In the heat of the moment, the mind selects and highlights certain details and omits other details. The angry mind is thoroughly convinced of its interpretations; that almost always requires blocking out contradictory evidence. When we're angry, we're like a lawyer trying to make the case that our anger is fully justified. To justify our case, we leave out certain details and emphasize others. When we actually can cool down through our mindfulness practice, the situation looks different. We find that there is some delusion bound up in our anger. Poet and philosopher Henry Wadsworth Longfellow's words are instructive: "If we could read the secret history of our enemies, we should find in each man's life, sorrow and suffering enough to disarm all hostility."

Investigating Anger

In the Buddhist tradition, anger has been described as having a *honeyed tip, but poisoned root.* We long for the sweetness of the honey, only to suffer from indigestion and regret. The honey of anger is real. When anger comes it makes a promise: "Act on this anger and I'll leave you alone; then you'll feel much better." When we follow our habit and act out the anger, we get a taste of the honey. The tension in our body and mind momentarily releases. It tastes sweet. But after the honey comes the poison—the painful consequences of our unconscious habits around anger. We harm others and ourselves. Our day is ruined; a relationship is harmed; we're filled with guilt or regret. When we sense the honey, we need to remember the poison and practice renouncing the sweetness.

Navigating anger skillfully depends on our curiosity and the sincerity of our investigation. What is anger? How does it arise in body and mind? Emotional experiences are not singular, irreducible events. They are composed of different aspects of experience: thoughts and emotional sensations (feelings) in the body. Thoughts can be further deconstructed into mental images and internally spoken words. Bringing awareness to each of these components of experience during episodes of anger builds our capacity for mindfulness and equanimity. This means that during the experience of anger, we can maintain mindful connection with emotional sensations in the body, mental images, and words.

How might this process actually look in practice? Let's say you are in a meeting and begin to feel frustrated and annoyed with a colleague's remarks. With mindfulness, you catch the signs that anger is present. You notice that your jaw is clenched and feel a strong impulse to make a harsh comment that will dismiss that person's point of view. Recognizing that anything you say out of that reactive state will not be productive, you set an intention to practice with the anger rather than acting on it. As you mindfully observe your experience, you notice a range of thoughts, sensations, and impulses come and go: contraction in your jaw and shoulders, an unpleasant tangle of sensations in your chest, images of the relief you might feel if you said something harsh, thoughts and memories justifying your position. You remember the harm that anger can cause, the guilt you might feel if you act out. You can almost taste the honey, but remember the poison. As you bear with the surges of intensity, they begin to fade. As the grip of the anger passes, you feel more space inside. You realize there is a way to ask a question that would express your concern and invite further discussion.

Reactivity arises out of the absence of mindfulness and equanimity. In the above example, if the intensity of one of those surges were stronger than the mindfulness at any given moment it could have overwhelmed the mind and tipped over into reactivity. When we are mindful, we don't act out our emotions but are informed by them. When we practice in this way, we are expanding our capacity to be free, even amidst intensity.

SUPPORTING ADOLESCENTS TO NAVIGATE ANGER

Your efforts to navigate anger in your own life expand the toolkit for supporting adolescents. When working with an adolescent who is angry, first try to honor the raw intensity of the experience itself. Your ability to make space for the emotion communicates to the young person that their emotions are acceptable and can be handled skillfully. Next, seek to understand the nature of the anger. This isn't about diagnosing the adolescent or pathologizing the anger, but really trying to understand its contours. If you've done your own work with anger, you will be less intimidated by it and more at ease discussing it. When you've trained yourself to be nondefensive, you can weather the storm even if some of the adolescent's anger is directed at you. To the extent that you have a prior relationship with the adolescent, you can leverage the goodwill that has been developed.

Bring forth a deep willingness to give attention to the adolescent and to try to understand things from their perspective. This means that you enter their realm of experience, asking questions and listening to the nuances of their experience. Examine the situation in a way that is least likely to create defensiveness on their part. In your words and manner, attune to tenderness and sensitivity. Even though anger resists vulnerability, we all experience anger because we can be hurt. In some sense, anger is an attempt to protect our heart against that very vulnerability.

Seek to calibrate the appropriateness of the anger. This can be a delicate assessment, especially if you do not have a trusting relationship with the individual or you fail to appreciate the distinctive experiences of a particular gender, racial, or ethnic identity. Do your best to respect these potential gaps of understanding. Is the anger a response to unfairness, mistreatment, or the adolescent being misconstrued in some way? Do concrete steps need to be taken to address the situation? If so, action might be necessary before any inner work can proceed. Until an appropriate boundary has been set, it is more challenging to navigate anger effectively.

This all requires patience. For a while, you might simply listen. Sometimes the venting process needs to run its course; just receiving their words can have a therapeutic effect. Use reflective statements that summarize what you hear. Sometimes, these reflective statements might translate the experience into language from the mindfulness or socioemotional learning realm. Aim to carefully restate what the adolescent says, gently reframing what is said in a way that will still resonate with the adolescent. Provide accurate empathy, but you may add some interpretation that will be empowering for the adolescent.

Often, in episodes of anger, some egoic wounding has happened. This is not invariably the case, but you can perceive how anger emerges out of threat to the sense of self. We have previously discussed the fragility of self-view during adolescence. This fragility makes for very fertile ground for anger. Acknowledging this form of pain that can accompany anger is important; navigate with care the sensitivities associated with egoic fragility. When you support a young person in navigating anger, find a balance between statements that support and strengthen a healthy sense of self and statements that help them acknowledge and feel any egoic wounding. The balance depends on the openness and stability of the adolescent.

When the adolescent feels sufficiently seen and heard, and when the intensity of the emotion has sufficiently de-escalated, they may be ready to explore the difference between the external stimulus and their internal response, beginning to take some responsibility for the experience of anger. You can gently introduce the perspectives of mindfulness that teach radical responsibility as a way of investigating their inner life. If the adolescent can do this, it will tend to further reduce the intensity of the anger and can lead to empowering insights into their own mind.

Rumination and other forms of obsessive thinking exacerbate anger. Adolescents and adults alike can get stuck in cycles where they are essentially reliving a painful experience in their own minds, again and again. This pattern can rekindle the flames of the anger, even when it has subsided and there is only the ember left. You can help the adolescent step out of rumination and experience the anger as it manifests in the body. This can often be detected along the front axis of the body—the face, throat, chest, and belly, and sometimes the hands. Explore the somatic manifestation of anger. Can the adolescent be aware of the constellation of sensations? Can they detect the pleasant or unpleasant character of the experience? Can they develop some measure of equanimity with it? You might coach them to soothe the anger by breathing slowly, filling up the belly, chest, and even the shoulders with the breath and then breathing out slowly. They might even envision the breath as soothing the sensations of anger. As the narrative of anger ceases to compel all of the attention, there tends to be an experience of more space inside and reduced intensity.

CONSIDER THIS . . .

Our ability to tolerate discomfort is often just one deep breath away. Your breath is something that is all yours, nobody can take it from you. Allow yourself these moments of freedom with each full breath.

SELF-HARSHNESS

We've been discussing the way anger can be directed outwards. Sometimes, that energy turns inwards with a tone of harshness, criticism, or self-hatred. This is all too common in adolescents, where heightened self-consciousness, perfectionism, and susceptibility to peer influence exacerbate questions of belonging. Some adolescents might rarely direct anger externally but treat themselves with contempt or even cruelty. The tendency toward negative self-talk can become so pervasive and entrenched that adolescents don't even realize it's an unhealthy habit they picked up along the way—a habit that can be changed. The mindful path through inwardly directed anger is different from the way to navigate outwardly directed anger. Here, self-compassion becomes especially relevant.

Self-compassion is as powerful a quality for adults as it is for adolescents. How many colleagues, teachers, or administrators do you know who struggle with self-care? How often do you sacrifice your own well-being for the demands of your profession? While the rewards of teaching can be profound, educators face job stresses that challenge the maintenance of emotional balance. Teachers are charged with creating a structured learning environment that promotes academic achievement, intellectual curiosity, and socioemotional development. Accountability to standardized learning outcomes intensifies the demands of teaching. Successfully meeting these objectives places a significant burden on teachers. For students, social and academic pressures weigh heavily. Self-judgment and painful social comparison create substantial burdens. For both educators and students, orienting toward self-care and self-compassion can be profoundly healing.

The philosopher, Martha Nussbaum (2002) counsels, "Do not despise your inner world. That is the first and most general piece of advice I would give to a generation . . ." (p. 176). She goes on to explain how our emotions are ultimately an expression of our vulnerability. This is valuable for adults to model and adolescents to understand.

> We all begin our lives as helpless babies, dependent on others for comfort, food, and survival itself. And even though we develop a degree of mastery and independence, we always remain alarmingly weak and incomplete, dependent on others and on an uncertain world for whatever we are able to achieve. As we grow, we all develop a wide range of emotions responding to this predicament: fear that bad things will happen and that we will be powerless to ward them off; love for those who help and support us; grief when a loved one is lost; hope for good things in the future; anger when someone else damages something we care about. *Our emotional life maps our incompleteness: A*

creature without any needs would never have reasons for fear, or grief, or hope, or anger. For that very reason we are often ashamed of our emotions and of the relations of need and dependency bound up with them. (p. 176–177)

Our emotions map our incompleteness. Emotions, in other words, signal our deepest human needs. This understanding highlights the importance of self-compassion for navigating the full range of our emotional lives.

The Terrain of Self-Harshness

It may be easier to understand self-compassion by first considering its opposite. The psychologist who refined the concept of self-compassion, Kristin Neff and Roos Vonk (2009), describe self-harshness in this way:

Although people typically value being kind and compassionate to others, they are often harsh and uncaring toward themselves. The intense self-focus that occurs when people confront their own limitations can sometimes lead to a type of tunnel vision in which people become overidentified with and carried away by negative thoughts and feelings about themselves. Feelings of isolation can also occur when people temporarily forget that failure and imperfection are part of the shared human experience, serving to amplify and exacerbate suffering. (p. 26)

Although some rare folks may be largely free of self-doubt and consistently kind toward themselves, many of us treat ourselves more harshly than we treat others. This harshness can show up in different ways. Often, it comes in the form of intense negative thought patterns of self-judgment. Sometimes, there is a strand of perfectionism, where our own fallibility is met with rigid control. We may feel a great deal of anxiety about performing successfully and strive to maintain our self-image. Many feel shame or embarrassment when failing to meet the expectations imposed by family, culture, or society.

Another way this self-harshness can manifest is through a lack of self-confidence and low self-esteem. Teens so often hear what they're not good at that they frequently internalize the voice of self-doubt and carry it into their attempts at mindfulness practice. "I can't do this . . . I'm no good at mindfulness . . . I don't know anything about that . . ." Jozen Tamori Gibson notes that some of the teens he works with undercut themselves each time after they speak saying, "Nah, never mind . . . I don't know what I'm talking about . . ."

However we arrive there, in a moment of self-harshness we are confronted by our imperfections, our foibles, the limitations of our control and will—and the heart closes. We forget that in those moments we're actually having an important insight about the human condition: we're imperfect. Facing challenges, life either softens or hardens the heart. Mindfulness training, whether for ourselves as educators or for the adolescents in our classrooms, prepares us so that in these moments, instead of closing, the heart relaxes and we learn something about being human.

Mindfulness opens the doorway to beginning to understand the levers and mechanisms of self-harshness. Sometimes, we're harsh with ourselves as a strategy to motivate ourselves to reach some goal or accomplishment. Maybe we don't like how we performed or feel disappointed by how we handled a situation with a student. The tone of the internal voice changes and all of a sudden our thinking is critical and sharp. It's almost as if we're running a small behavior modification program with ourselves, discouraging some behavior by introducing a negative experience. We are essentially punishing ourselves in an attempt to produce the desired behavior or outcome. This self-punishment is usually ineffective and comes at a high cost in well-being, quality of life, and morale.

Kristen Neff (2003) defines self-compassion as "being open to and moved by one's own suffering, experiencing feelings of caring and kindness toward oneself, taking an understanding, nonjudgmental attitude toward one's inadequacies and failures, and recognizing that one's experience is part of the common human experience" (p. 224). Crucially, Neff distinguishes self-compassion from self-esteem. In the past, there has been enthusiasm for school programs aimed at increasing self-esteem or a student's general evaluation of herself. However, research identified significant problems with the celebration of self-esteem, especially in the form of indiscriminate praise. Carol Dweck, a Stanford professor known for her work on mindset, has argued that "what students need the most is not self-esteem boosting or trait labeling; instead, they need mindsets that represent challenges as things that they can take on and overcome over time with effort, new strategies, learning, help from others, and patience" (Yeager & Dweck, 2012, p. 312). Self-compassion is not an *evaluation* of oneself based on particular outcomes or experiences, but a *relationship* to experience. It presents an alternative approach to developing the resilience and patience highlighted by Dweck.

Adolescence and Self-Compassion

Self-compassion is especially relevant for adolescents. As we've discussed, adolescents develop a sophisticated *theory of mind*, in which they are better able to conceptualize the internal states of oneself and others. As this capacity develops, more nuanced forms of self-consciousness blossom. The heightened sensitivity to peer evaluations places adolescents in a precarious position. Neff and McGehee (2010) summarize the predicament:

> The emotional difficulties of the teen years often stem from concerns with self-evaluation. Adolescents may ask themselves "Am I a worthy person?", "What do other people think of me?", or "Am I as good as others?" A continual process of self-evaluation and social comparison occurs as teens attempt to establish their identity and place in the social hierarchy. The intense pressures faced by most adolescents, such as stress over academic performance, the need to be popular and fit in

with the right peer crowd, issues of body image, concerns with sexual attractiveness, and so on, means that the self-evaluations of teens are often unfavorable. Negative self-judgments are strongly implicated in the high rates of anxiety, depression, and attempted suicide found during this period. (p. 225)

A recent meta-analysis of the relationship between self-compassion and psychological distress that looked at 19 studies featuring over 7000 participants found a strong inverse relationship between psychological distress (e.g., anxiety, depression, stress) and self-compassion among adolescents (Marsh, Chan, & MacBeth, 2018). In other words, the higher the self-compassion, the lower the distress. The authors conclude that self-compassion may be an important factor to target in interventions supporting adolescent emotional well-being.

In our own work, we've found that adolescents are especially receptive to lessons on self-compassion. When the topic is introduced, they reflexively feel the acute pain of self-judgment and social pressure. Provided enough emotional trust has been created with the group, teens will readily acknowledge the ubiquitous and painful effects of these social forces. (Recall the student from Chapter 5 who remarked, "*I never knew that you all judged yourself. I feel really happy to know I'm not the only one judging myself.*") They long for social settings where they are bonded by their sensitivity, rather than by its concealment.

As with mindfulness, introducing the practice of self-compassion begins with establishing relevance. There are many creative ways to do this. One persuasive approach is to engage in a discussion that articulates the challenges of being an adolescent for a particular group of teens. These must be their concerns, rather than the concerns adults might have about the adolescents. For some students, perfectionism and the relentless pressure to perform academically, engage in extracurricular activities, and gain admission to a particular university may be a heavy burden. For others, the pressure to fit in socially or accept certain aspects of themselves may be painful. The struggle to acknowledge the pain or limitations of one's family or of our society may be especially poignant. Highlighting the universality of these difficulties is one pathway into kindness practices.

Similar to introducing mindfulness, another pathway is to highlight the benefits of kindness or compassion. Begin a dialogue defining the meaning of these terms in order to establish a shared language. Invite students to reflect on how it feels to be on the receiving end of kindness and compassion. Debate the perennial question of human nature and explore the value of these qualities in our relationships, families, communities, and society. Challenge your students to consider the contrast between their readiness to be kind to others and their willingness to direct care toward themselves.

> **TRY THIS . . .**
> Dyad exercise to celebrate what we like about ourselves!
> Partner up. Each person has three uninterrupted minutes to tell their partner what they like about themselves. This isn't always easy, yet this is an opportunity to celebrate and see what we do like. Once both participants have gone, bring the group back together. Each partner, with permission, will tell three things that their partner likes about themselves to the whole group. Ask the kids to do this regularly for themselves so that they can begin to develop a kindness practice towards themselves.

Three Ways Kindness Practices Work

Within the framework of mindfulness training, self-compassion is often considered a *heartfulness* practice, together with the cultivation of other positive states like kindness, gratitude, and generosity. These heart practices can function in at least three different ways. When sharing these practices with teens and adolescents, having a clear and thorough understanding of how they function (from direct experience) provides essential perspectives and information to guide students in the practice.

1. **Cultivating.** When we cultivate kindness, self-compassion, or any other positive mind state, we are evoking a particular emotional state, typically through the use of phrases or images. For example, we might silently repeat a simple phrase to ourselves such as, "May I meet my limitations with kindness and compassion." It's as if we ring the bell of self-compassion in the mind and then listen to its reverberations in the heart and body. In this way, we create an internal reference point of care and kindness. It is pleasant to rest in these states, which become more accessible over time. With practice, it becomes possible to immediately drop the distress of a moment of harshness and return to a felt sense of one's innate goodness. Over the course of months and years, this creates a sense of inner refuge. It is as if the heart is never far away.

2. **Concentrating.** Sometimes, heartfulness practice produces no discernible affective reaction—we experience no juicy feelings of tenderness or love. Instead, the circuits of the emotional body are quiet. We try evoking a feeling of kindness or compassion, but feel nothing. This can be dispiriting if we're unable to contextualize the experience. Sometimes, this flatness is merely a phase that gives way to positive feeling. Other times, it can be used to deepen concentration. Instead of focusing on our emotional response, we use the phrases to gather the attention. We pour all of our awareness into the words, relinquishing the notion that we're supposed to feel any particular way. The mind can collect around these words and become very quiet. It is almost as if the circuits required for chatter in the mind are partially recruited to utter the phrases of kindness. This quiet can be subtly pleasant, deeply soothing, or even rapturously delightful. There can be a sense of protection and seclusion within the phrases and the inner quiet their repetition produces. This can't be

engineered, but it does unfold over the course of practice. Students who do not experience feelings of warmth can be encouraged to notice any relative tranquility and gather all of their attention behind the words. This can provide a sense of refuge from the relentless distractibility of the mind and the stress of change.

3. **Metabolizing.** Sometimes, it is said that heartfulness practice acts like a magnet, bringing to the surface its opposites, such as the forces of shame, anger, resentment, or sadness. Many people begin heartfulness practice and encounter these potent, difficult feelings. Again, without a context to understand these experiences, adults and students alike will often interpret it as evidence that they are failing or practicing incorrectly. However, these experiences are a normal and completely appropriate part of the unfolding of heartfulness practice. The difficulty is actually an opening—there's a crack in the self-critical façade, which makes room for self-compassion to enter. The heart is learning kindness and compassion by tasting their opposites.

For many adolescents, the path of self-compassion entails a measure of grieving as they open to the pain of self-harshness. The experience of self-kindness can punctuate the pain of self-harshness that has shaped their lives. They grieve the harm they've done to themselves, the harm they've done to others, or the harm others have done to them. Old losses may to come to the surface. They even may begin to grieve the difficulties inherent to the human condition: how we all long to be safe and happy but can't always make it so.

Students may not even recognize they are grieving. As instructors, we can support them to weather these storms and help them reframe the pain as a natural prelude to more insight, kindness, and emotional freedom. In metabolizing difficult states, we bring a spirit of nonviolence to the emotions and memories that arise. We're not turning any experience into an enemy. Hating our struggles just compounds the problem. As one meditation teacher, Shinzen Young (2016), said, we love our difficulties to death.

These experiences of grief are not restricted to self-compassion practice. In fact, grieving is a facet of mindfulness more generally. How do we develop compassion and insight? How do we let go? Experientially, the development of kindness and deeper understanding entails relinquishing our illusions and encountering what's incomplete in our own hearts. We often experience this as an emotion akin to grief. As we come to see the poignancy of our longing to be happy, being gentle with ourselves feels more and more natural. Alluding to the connections between grief and love, Mother Teresa famously commented, "May God break my heart so completely that the whole world falls in." Importantly, this process of grieving is not bottomless. We can metabolize our life and meet the human condition wholeheartedly, such that nothing feels left out of the heart.

CHAPTER 8

NAVIGATING PLEASURES AND DISTRACTIONS: TECHNOLOGY, SEX, AND SUBSTANCES

By the time I'd hit my young teens I was seriously disconnected from my internal world. My upper-middle-class professional parents divorced when I was ten. I bounced back and forth between households and their often unhealthy relationships. I was trying to fit into all-white communities as a biracial black child, and I had no one to talk to about my feelings. My best counselors were other kids as confused as myself. Numbing out and fitting in, to the best of my immature ability, was the only way I knew how to survive in the world of my peers. They, too, were grappling with their bodies, hormones, and social and family issues; they didn't have wise choices or answers but knew ways to escape through drugs, alcohol, and sex. What we had in common was our desire to forget the pain in our lives. The alternative was heartache, loneliness, confusion, and loss.

AS HUMANS, THE WAY WE CONSUME IS IN DIRECT relationship to what is going on around us individually, communally, socially, politically, and globally. At times of abundance, we tend to celebrate, purchase, and enjoy the available pleasures. In times of difficulty, we tend to grow anxious, numb out, and try to find ways to escape or forget. These behavioral patterns have been a reality for humans throughout time; they're one of the reasons that Shakespeare became popular. Theatre and laughter gave the poor and destitute public a way to forget their poverty, rampant disease, and death. Similarly, the ancient Romans found the executions and gladiatorial contests held in the Colosseum entertaining in all their gruesome glory.

Distracting ourselves with entertainment to cope is a part of our human legacy. We seek ways to avoid and escape our uncomfortable experiences and to celebrate and enhance our pleasurable ones. Our students share these same desires. In this chapter, we will look at the most common options adolescents today have to distract themselves: drugs, alcohol, sex, social media, video games, and other technology. These behaviors in and of themselves are the topics of entire books, but we'll explore them here with a view to how mindfulness practices can aid in mitigating unnecessary harm. Of course, this is not exclusively an issue for teenagers; adults often lean on substances or harmful practices that enable us to separate from experiences that are difficult or scary. How we understand and relate to these substances and activities can make the difference between a meaningful and productive life, and a downward spiral into pain and addiction.

A caveat: please do not mistake this chapter as a way to deal with addiction or any potential serious harm. Although mindfulness is a beneficial additive to other mental and emotional health treatment, it is not a panacea. This chapter is merely an introduction to how we as educators, parents, and others who work with and care about young people can help adolescents engage with mindfulness as a healthier coping mechanism.

THE NATURALNESS OF DISTRACTION

In exploring this topic, we don't want to demonize the natural curiosity adolescents have for fun, pleasure, and connection. Those who have spent time with toddlers are all too familiar with their seemingly endless store of *why* questions and the tactile curiosity they express about everything within their environment. It is at times cute or annoying (depending on our mood); yet for them this curiosity is a necessity for figuring out the world in which they are living. When those same toddlers grow into adolescents and young adults, they are still trying to assess their environments, figure out where they are safe, and learn how to belong. The noted pediatrician and developmental researcher, Ronald Dahl (2004), has commented that the adolescent brain is extremely well-adapted for one of its central purposes: to explore and learn. Developmental curiosities can lead to significant growth and exploration but if misguided, they can take us off the path of a fulfilling, connected, and productive life. The enticing elements of intoxicants take students down a path that can feel temporarily wise and useful; yet seeking long-term ease from these can lead to missing out on genuine human connections and an experience of real depth in life.

Many adolescents are wise and have strong survival instincts. We as adults have a lot to learn from their raw wisdom. Yet adolescents' instinct for survival can also be a problem, especially when that instinct tells them to fit in at all costs. Belonging to a tribe and feeling that they are part of a peer group can cause students to act in ways that might not be their natural inclination; it can feel like life or death in their young minds to survive and thrive socially. The question for them arises, "Will I belong and be accepted, or will I be an outcast?"

JoAnna is the mother of three, grandmother of one. While raising her kids, their house was often a fun, safe place to hang out as well as a spiritual center for many kids in the neighborhood. In her words:

> *Young people seem to find it safe to talk to me, and this position has allowed me to be in the middle of many wise and unwise choices. I've seen kids who seem to be the most balanced of all get pulled off track. I've seen kids that have grown up in close families, attended good schools, and enjoyed emotional health decide that trying methamphetamine with close friends would be a fun experience or think that pilfering the Valium in their parents' med-*

icine cabinet would be a good addition to their friend's party. There are also kids who are socially positioned in unstable, painful, and traumatic life situations, who have a need to feel normal *for a little while and turn toward substances for that shift.*

These desires to use are natural and not occasions for judgment or shaming. Yet as adults, it is incumbent on us as the caretakers of our youth to intervene. When JoAnna's 2 1/2-year-old grandson thinks it's a glorious idea to jump in the swimming pool unattended, even though he doesn't know how to swim, we let him know that that is a terrible and life-threatening decision. We also take the steps necessary to teach him how to swim. As an intervention, mindfulness can be compared to those swimming lessons. Mindfulness is an excellent way of getting to the root causes of why young people look outside themselves and turn to substances or other activities to distract, numb out, or fit in, instead of the more difficult task of looking inward.

Our hope, as grown-up young people—as adults who care about youngsters—is that we can help them and be there in times of experimentation, confusion, change, loss, and all of the situations that we, even as adults, find it difficult to navigate. We are part of the story that brings our children to external substances, not separate from it. When we separate ourselves from their story, we lose touch with how we can find empathy and understanding for what they are going through.

When we take on mindfulness practice we build personal as well as relational wisdom. As we continue to practice mindfulness, momentum builds, and we tend to make healthier choices. We become more attuned to our emotional world as well as to how those around us are engaging with their emotions. When we are aware of our inner life, we tend to align our external choices more wisely and honestly. As humans, we know that we like to feel good and we also know that an unchecked pursuit of pleasure can cause serious harm. Holding mindfulness as a core practice can guide us on a path of nonharm for both ourselves and others.

Distractions and Addictions: Being the Adult in the Room

Adults, of course, aren't always wiser than adolescents. Media and peer influence are not the only ways that students are exposed to alcohol, drugs, sex, and self-harm. Kids are constantly watching and paying attention to the adults in their lives. We, too, play a big part in what become norms for kids through modeling. As mindful adults, we need to think about how we engage with these substances ourselves and recognize that what we do and how we communicate about what we do has an impact on the young people in our lives. As an example, I've often been at social events or restaurants and witnessed adults who have been drinking hop in the car with their children and drive off. It's hypocritical to ask our youth not to drink and drive when they are watching adults around them do it. Adults too often want to blame our children for their missteps and mistakes, without looking at how their own actions or broader systems play into the behaviors that trickle down to our children. If we can engage in open and trusting dialogue with young people about the behaviors that can be a way to cope and fit in or to rebel—use of drugs and alcohol, unhealthy sexual relationships, addiction to social media, self-harm—we may be able to connect with them in ways that will feel more impactful and useful than anything they can experience from external stimuli.

MEDIA BOMBARDMENT AND SOCIETAL PRESSURE

Becoming aware about what we ingest in the media and how it can affect us is a crucial tipping point in the mindfulness practice. In the contemporary world of global media, we are all exposed to images and information that continually challenge our nervous systems and minds. Immersion in social media puts us in a state of comparing, challenging, competing, and often arguing with these images and statuses that we scroll through rapidly—taking it all in and responding at a pace that is too rapid to digest. Young people are exposed to the so-called glamour of skinny people drinking beer at a football game, edgy reality shows where heroin and crystal meth use are a way to find freedom from the confines of parental rules, comedies where getting stoned out of your mind and pulling crazy stunts gives relief to a hard day. The news, full of violent and shocking events, puts our kids on the defense, feeling the need to fight or fix. There was a time when going to school felt safe, but no longer. There was a time when going to a house of worship was safe; this safety is now challenged. There was a time when going to dance clubs or concerts was fun and free; unfortunately, this all now comes with internal wariness and anxiety. The constant catastrophes happening to people their age—and the instant, traumatic media reportage of them—has a cumulative impact on their nervous systems. Even while there are positive trends in terms of violence globally, public perception is often that things are getting worse. As young people, the need for relief becomes even stronger when many of the spaces that they felt were sacred or exciting no longer hold that appeal or promise of relief. Nowadays, there is a perpetual edge of stress, anxiety, and worry that teens carry, even if unconsciously.

Adults have fully developed nervous systems. While we aren't always great at coping, either, most of us know what loss, sorrow, grief, social anxiety, and boundaries feel like. We've found ways, especially if we consider ourselves mindfulness practitioners, to handle that which unsettles us. Adolescents don't quite have that skill set yet. Getting high or drunk is a quick, easy fix to an overstimulated system. It's easier to forget or blow off steam than to work with strong feelings on one's own.

This landscape is complicated by the centrality of technology generally, and social media specifically, in the lives of adolescents. Both mindfulness and technology are about attention. The persuasive design that animates much of technology is trying to keep you glued to your phone as long as possible. Mindfulness is about being right where you are, in this moment, and then choosing consciously where you place your attention.

Attention is our most basic human currency and it is worthy of protection.

Attention is a limited resource. How technology fragments or enhances our attention is a critical investigation. Often, we find that the pull of technology overpowers us. On average, people check their phone 150 times per day. Tristan Harris, former design ethicist at Google and cofounder of The Center for Humane Technology, is bringing more awareness to problematic effects of an "extractive attention economy." Technology companies' valuation depend on the level of engagement of their customers. This means that the more time people spend on a particular device or app, the more valuable the company becomes. This incentivizes engineering for ultimate compulsivity. Harris holds up a phone and says, "This thing is a slot machine" (60 Minutes, 2018) The unpredictability of winning stimulates our desire to check again and again, making our device more addictive. Apps create special sounds and icons for notifications; YouTube autoplays more videos to keep us from leaving; Instagram shows new "likes" one at a time—all to keep us checking for more. Facebook algorithms are designed to show whatever keeps us scrolling. Snapchat turns conversations into streaks we don't want to lose. The media turns events into breaking news to keep us watching.

Research on the effects of high technological use in adults and in adolescents is just emerging, but there are some strong preliminary warning signs. For example, Kross and colleagues (2013) found that Facebook usage was associated with declines in well-being. He concludes:

> The human need for social connection is well established, as are the benefits that people derive from such connections. On the surface, Facebook provides an invaluable resource for fulfilling such needs by allowing people to instantly connect. Rather than enhancing well-

being, as frequent interactions with supportive "offline" social networks powerfully do, the current findings demonstrate that interacting with Facebook may predict the opposite result for young adults—it may undermine it. (p. 5)

Subsequent research has fleshed out these findings. Fox and Moreland (2015) write that, while Facebook users often experience negative emotion while on the site, the fear of missing out or losing connection with peers promotes more compulsive use. Researchers have highlighted a difference between active and passive use. While active usage refers to direct exchanges with others (e.g., posting status updates, commenting on posts), passive usage is the consumption of information without any direct exchanges. It appears that passive Facebook usage may be more closely associated with compromised well-being than active usage. Verduyn and colleagues (2015) found that passive Facebook use led to a decline in well-being and that this decline was due to increased envy. The tendency to compare ourselves to others and define ourselves through our relative status is stimulated by social media. The platforms capitalize on human vulnerabilities, especially adolescent vulnerabilities, to make us more compulsive.

> **CONSIDER THIS . . .**
> *Going on a social media fast can be an illuminating experience for a group of adolescents. Choose one day and collectively commit to abstain from social media. When you re-gather, explore what was missed and any relief that may be have been experienced.*

Not all effects of technology or social media are negative. Nor is it clear what role mindfulness will have in mitigating the problems. As Harris points out, there are thousands of gifted engineers working all the time to design ways to keep us glued to our screens. Some of the solutions will require new technological designs that aim to meet our needs, rather than to exploit our vulnerabilities. For adolescents, mindfulness may not be sufficiently developed to counter the intense appeal of devices. Nevertheless, the stability and clarity of mindfulness is a powerful contrast with the compulsive and automatic process that typifies much of our engagement with technology, holding promise for supporting the younger generation to exercise more choice and awareness around their relationships to social media and technology in general.

Initiate honest conversations about what teens appreciate and dislike about technology. They may hear themselves express concerns that catalyze a wish to change their relationship with it. Here are a few simple questions to get students thinking and spark conversation about how they interface with technology.

+ How many have ever sent a message to someone online that you wouldn't say to that person directly?
+ How many have ever felt ashamed, hurt, angry, or embarrassed by something someone else posted or said about them online?
+ Raise your hand if you ever feel like the adults in your life spend more time paying attention to their phone than to you?
+ Who here has stayed up late online only to regret in the morning?
+ What's it like to spend time with friends who are glued to their phones?
+ What's your favorite thing about your cell phone or other device? Your least favorite?

Get creative in creating and exploring mindfulness practice with a device. Have students practice being mindful of their internal experience seeing their phone face down on their desk, picking it up, turning it on, seeing a notification, and so forth.

The Center for Humane Technology (www.humanetech.com) suggests that a healthy relationship with technology will only emerge through ethical technology design, regulation, and media pressure. Nevertheless, it offers some practical suggestions for managing compulsive technology use that can protect our attention:

- Turn off notifications; only use notifications for people trying to reach you.
- Limit the home screen to tools, things you use for tasks like Maps, Camera, or Calendar.
- Move the rest of your apps off the first page and into folders. That way you only look at them when you want, rather than opening them just because you see them.
- Charge your device outside your bedroom, or use an alarm clock to wake up.
- Track the time you spend on your device with an app.
- Set your phone to grayscale since the bright colors are visually compelling.
- Remove social media from your phone.
- Send audio notes rather than texting.

SEXUAL URGES AND CHOICES

Sexuality is at the forefront of media and social media, and it is one of the strongest distractions to which adolescents are prone. At a developmental stage when they are dealing with raging hormones, longing for intimacy, and struggling with how to find meaningful relationships in the era of *hooking up*, they are also bombarded by sexual conversations and images portrayed by artists and celebrities, with news about the #MeToo movement, discussions around consent, and the political rights of women's bodies. By the time we hit early puberty, our hormones and bodies are telling us that we're ready for sex. For approximately 200,000 years our human ancestors mated when their bodies were hormonally ready. Simply put, young bodies are biologically ready for sex, even as emotional and psychological complexity abounds. The evolution of human sexuality and thought has created a bind for many of us between what the body is telling us, what the heart is telling us, and how the norms of society affect us.

The classroom is a perfect opportunity for courageous and much needed adult voices to engage students in these kinds of conversations through books, art, history, science, and the creative use of media. JoAnna's daughter went to an all-girls Catholic school. One of her favorite classes (and therefore favorite teachers) was a class called "Love and Choices." This class gave girls an opportunity to talk with their teacher and each other about issues that they face daily as young women. They were introduced to literature and films that helped them think deeply about dating, celibacy, objectification of women in the media, and theories such as Maslow's hierarchy of needs. She came home with questions and a desire to continue the conversation about Audre Lorde's *Sister Outsider*, Toni Morrison's *Song of Solomon*, and Charlotte Brontë's *Jane Eyre*, to name a few. She learned about the history of relationships in her history courses that spoke of marriage as a duty to the family, not love. When we can engage with young people in a direct and honest way, versus having them be educated on the streets, we have more influence over helping them make informed choices based on internal knowing rather than external influence.

Mythology is another fantastic teaching tool for having conversations with young people about the power of sex and sexuality. Aristophanes' Greek comedy, "Lysistrata," asks us to look at how sex holds political power, while the Persephone myth examines the relationship between disempowerment and oppression in sexual relationships. These are rich and potent conversations to explore with adolescents, who are actively grappling with these issues in their day-to-day lives. To support having these conversations in a safe and open way, consider creating separate groups based on gender for parts of the discussion. (And, don't assume that there only two genders!)

Sadly there are very few young people who have adults to talk to openly about their relationship to their sexuality. Most adolescents are getting their information from other kids their age or from pornography. Without the space and support to explore what's happening, the options are limited. When sensations of lust or longing arise, gratification seems like the best response. That might be appropriate at some times and not at others. As we know, mindlessly acting out one's sexual desire can have many long-term consequences like pregnancy, sexually transmitted disease, disconnection from our emotions, addiction to pornography, and infidelity. When we as adults can help adolescents get connected to what is going on, personally as well as socially, we offer them a great gift. We offer the gift of being able to feel good about their bodies and their relationships to them. When kids are connected to what is going on emotionally, they have a choice. With that choice comes the freedom to act out of wisdom and love.

SUBSTANCE USE

Adolescence is a sensitive period for neuropsychological development and simultaneously the peak period when substance use is initiated. Although many adolescents experiment with substances without enduring negative consequences, heavy use may disrupt brain development or emotional or interpersonal functioning. In exploring this terrain, it's helpful to understand that the choices young people make depend, in part, on their broader social and familial context. There are many risk factors that can predispose an adolescent to an unhealthy relationship with drugs and alcohol. These include parental conflict or separation, a family history of substance abuse, a history of maltreatment, trauma, drug availability, or stressful life events. Similarly, there is a range of factors that can protect kids against substance abuse, including parental health, active adult engagement and monitoring, and a supportive school environment. This all means that some adolescents may be at relatively low risk for serious negative effects of substance experimentation, while others may be impacted substantially. We also acknowledge the potential therapeutic benefits of substances. This is not a realm for moralism, but empiricism.

Our society's broader relationship with substances is another key factor in adolescents' experience around drugs and alcohol. For example, at the time of writing this book, cannabis is legal in 11 states in the United States and broadly available elsewhere. Approximately 40% of 12th graders report having used cannabis at some point in the past year, according to the Monitoring the Future national survey (Johnston et al., 2019). The approach of strict prohibition is not effective and is likely to drive adolescents away from engagement with adults and more completely into their own peer group. As an adult supporting adolescents, you can serve primarily as a stable figure who is open to honest conversation, who is not moralistic, and who is sincerely invested in their welfare.

Many kids we've worked with have lost interest in doing anything other than isolating and getting high. School work ceases; relationships deteriorate; eventually, just about anything else they may have been interested in can be lost. These kids, in the grip of completely checking out, often have no coping skills to engage with what they may be experiencing. In circumstances like this, reprimands and punishment aren't helpful. Just as mindfulness asks us to move in close to our internal experience, this is a time for elders and mentors in adolescents' lives to move in closer, with compassion.

While it is beyond the scope of this book to describe the role of mindfulness in treating substance abuse, we can make some general points. Mindfulness can function as a stress-reduction technique, which may be helpful in reducing the urge to use substances. The practice is also associated with decreased impulsivity, another protective factor in substance use. What's more, the moment-to-moment attention developed by mindfulness practice may buffer against painful memories of the past or the ruminative concerns of the future. Mindfulness also helps us develop equanimity with urges and other unpleasant experiences. As we describe in Chapter 9, mindfulness functions as a kind of *exposure therapy*, desensitizing us to unpleasant feelings, and thereby reduces the tendency to react automatically. This is thought to be one mechanism through which mindfulness buffers adolescents against substance misuse.

HOW MINDFULNESS CAN HELP

As we explored in Chapter 5, regardless of whether you are working in a juvenile detention facility or a fancy private school, many young people feel that they are the only ones experiencing discomfort or unease, whatever form that may take: internal confusion, doubt, emotional or physical insecurity, school stress, social anxiety, parental and peer conflict, and so on. This feeling is incredibly lonely and can cause kids to isolate, pull inward, or avoid their emotions instead of reaching out, getting closer, and becoming more vulnerable or intimate. When our thoughts and emotions are overwhelming, mindfulness practice invites us to look more deeply at our direct experience and to question our assumptions and beliefs.

A few years ago, JoAnna was running a group at a male juvenile detention facility, working with some young men who had had difficult lives. These young men were hardened because forces in their environment—society, their neighborhoods, their parents, their schools—had not made it easy to function as emotional beings. They would not have survived had they allowed themselves to feel and express their emotions. When she would ask them what a feeling was, they'd share a thought instead, "It's like when you wanna beat someone up," or "It's like when you just wanna take something without paying." They offered lots of mental similes and action steps, but never the core emotion that would provoke them wanting to act in a certain way. Similarly, when working with young girls who are always worried about what people think of them, they talk about wanting to get skinny or buy a particular clothing item so that they can fit in, yet they don't speak about loneliness or fear of being left out. In both examples, there is no connection to the motivation behind their action or behavior.

Knowing our emotional inner world is a crucial component of wise choices. When we feel sad, does that mean we check out with alcohol? When we feel lonely, does that mean that to feel better we need to hook up with someone we don't care about or who doesn't care about us? When we feel angry or anxious, does it mean we need to smoke some weed? At times, those can feel like the only options to adolescents, maybe even the reasonable choice.

If we listen to our students carefully and don't get too caught up in what we think they *should* be doing or how they *should* be behaving, we can be far better mentors, parents, educators, and advisors. The classroom is full of creative ways to engage in dialogue without being too annoyingly obvious. Art, literature, music, history, science, dance, and sports are all useful entry points for these discussions. Combining these topics with mindfulness tools provides a rich framework for discussing challenging, real-life issues and the emotional content that they provoke. Through investigation, dialogue, and skillful facilitation, we can help adolescents to recognize the strength and power of their own immediate awareness in navigating this terrain.

When young people choose to commit to a mindfulness practice and when they have other people in their life with whom they can share that, a natural next step is often for them to show up for life in a connected way. When we make a conscious choice to pay attention to how we feel internally, we are likely to pay more attention to how we think about, behave in, and experience our external world. Our actions, thoughts, and feelings will tend to include our friends, parents, siblings, and teachers as well as the planet. If we remain numb and disconnected through unhealthy and uninformed use of external substances or behaviors, it's much harder to see how we affect those around us as well as ourselves. As humans, we need social connection and some experience of the sacred—connection to something larger than ourselves. If we have no references or resources to connect, we will search on a more superficial level for meaning. We will try to string together moments of ease, joy, and peace through external sources in the hope that if we string enough of those moments together, we can finally be happy. Mindfulness reminds us that connection and sacredness are possible within, that the road there is through presence, and that it takes some work to travel down that path.

CHAPTER 9

TRAUMA, MINDFULNESS, AND MITIGATING HARM

At a 5-day mindfulness retreat with 40 teenagers, two girls disclosed to staff a history of sexual victimization. When kids trust adults, such disclosures are sadly common, and they can raise issues (such as duty to report suspected abuse, depending on the circumstances and the jurisdiction) and entail complications that are beyond the scope of this volume to address. We're familiar with these kinds of revelations, the pain and sometimes relief that follows in their wake. We do all we can to provide the emotional safety that lessens the burden of such memories. At this particular retreat, the group was notably kind and caring. The sense of self-consciousness that is so pervasive in adolescence had largely melted away, creating a deeper kind of relaxation. On the last night of the retreat, New Year's Eve, we held a ceremony focused on intentions for the new year and stayed up late. After midnight, the kids DJ'ed their own dance party. What followed was one of the most moving moments of my life. I was watching the group dancing, and noticed the two girls who had disclosed trauma earlier. They were dancing in a group, looking fully at ease, reveling in the music, held by the safety of friendship. They were enjoying each other, enjoying a forum where vigilance and self-consciousness was entirely unnecessary. They were getting to be kids.

THE WORD ITSELF, TRAUMA, IS EVOCATIVE, DERIVING FROM THE GREEK FOR "wound." In recent years there has been an increase in attention to the psychological wounds that can be inflicted by traumatic events and chronic stress, among the population at large but also to a troubling degree among school-age children. Within the discourse of mindfulness, concepts of trauma are playing an increasingly prominent role. Some of the emphasis on trauma is necessary and a corrective to a neglected subject. For too long, our society has been ignorant of, dismissive toward, or minimizing of the consequences of trauma. This is a tragic oversight, leaving those suffering without adequate support or understanding. The pendulum can also swing in the other direction. It is possible to overestimate the destructive effects of trauma and underestimate our resilience. In this chapter, we will examine trauma and its intersection with mindfulness: how trauma is defined, its prevalence, its range of consequences, and how trauma intersects with emotion regulation. We'll consider the question of whether or not mindfulness can cause harm and suggest tailored mindfulness interventions for traumatized adolescents.

In an important article, psychologist Nick Haslam (2016) describes how in recent decades certain negative concepts such as *mental disorder, addiction,* and *trauma* have become more elastic and expanded to include multiple phenomena under one umbrella. In the 1980s, the field of psychiatry defined a traumatic event as an event outside the range of usual human experience and something that would evoke symptoms of distress in almost anyone. In subsequent decades, this definition has been defined down—that is, broadened significantly to include a wide range of experiences. As Haslam states, current definitions have expanded dramatically and suggest that "a traumatic event need not be a discrete event, need not involve serious threats to life or limb, need not be outside normal experience, need not be likely to create marked distress in almost everyone, and need not even produce marked distress in the traumatized person, who must merely experience it as 'harmful.' Under this definition the concept of trauma is rendered much broader and more subjective than it was even three decades ago" (p. 2).

This kind of *concept creep* can obscure important facts about trauma. The role of trauma as a cause of psychological distress can be overestimated, and the role of resilience and the human capacity for successful adaptation in the face of challenge can be underestimated. Overstating the fragility of adolescents carries risk, just as denying vulnerability carries risk. As trauma therapies become increasingly prominent in our culture generally and within mindfulness communities specifically, it has been striking to observe this concept creep unfolding. Trauma is increasingly cited by adolescents and adults who are seeking to understand the suffering in their lives. While we fully acknowledge that this is appropriate in some cases, it can also be misguided in others. One of the attractions of invoking trauma as the primary cause of one's psychological or emotional pain is that it diffuses shame. This, of course, is a wonderful thing. Avoiding shame and destigmatizing distress is essential to the healing process. All too often, emotional pain is interpreted as a personal failing, as evidence of brokenness. This harshness is maladaptive and only compounds the pain. Are there problems in designating a wider and wider range of events trauma? In sharing mindfulness with adolescents, what is our responsibility to understand trauma and what can be learned about trauma and its consequences from the best available evidence?

WHAT ARE THE SOURCES OF TRAUMA, AND WHO IS AFFECTED?

It's an unfortunate fact that potentially traumatic experiences (PTE) are not rare, and a majority of teens have been exposed to at least one. One of the most prominent studies, in which over 6000 adolescents, aged 13 through 17 years, were surveyed, found that 62% of adolescents reported at least one PTE (McLaughlin et al., 2013). Twenty-nine percent reported a single PTE, 14% reported two PTEs and 19% reported three or more PTEs. The most common PTEs were the unexpected death of a loved one (28%), disasters (15%), and witnessing a death or serious injury (12%).

In another prominent study (Copeland, Keeler, Angold, & Costello, 2007), 1420 children between the ages of 9 and 13 years were assessed over a period of several years. Sixty-eight percent of the sample had experienced a PTE by age 16, with 37% experiencing two or more PTEs. Six percent of the adolescents had experienced a PTE in the previous 3 months. These data are consistent with earlier efforts to catalogue PTEs in childhood, such as the Adverse Childhood Experience Study (Felitti et al., 1998).

Typically, we think about trauma as the product of bad luck or a random occurrence. While this can be the case, an important finding from trauma research is that exposure to PTEs is not random. Vulnerabilities in the adolescent, their family, or previous adverse experience increase the likelihood of subsequent exposure to PTEs. Further, low-income communities, communities of color, and other marginalized populations are more likely to experience trauma. This effectively means that risk generates more risk, sometimes creating a cumulative burden on the adolescent. (It also implicates the institutions and structures of our society, that often distribute resources and risk inequitably, compounding the vulnerability of some segments of the population.) Copeland and colleagues found that the risk for exposure to PTEs was one in eight for the most advantaged children, but more than one in two for the most vulnerable youth. For example, adolescents with behavioral problems (conduct and oppositional behavior) are at elevated risk of being exposed to PTEs. The impulsivity and risk taking that characterizes youth with behavioral problems creates more opportunities to be exposed to PTEs. The cumulative burden of these risks can lead to a range of difficulties in life, from poor health to unemployment, from psychological and emotional distress to failed relationships and many other negative outcomes.

Exposure to an event generally does not do damage all on its own. Instead, research suggests that PTEs intersect with preexisting vulnerabilities to compromise functioning or lead to psychological symptoms. In other words, potentially traumatic experiences don't affect all adolescents the same way. Those who have previously had adverse experiences or have a history of psychiatric distress are substantially more likely to exhibit psychological symptoms following exposure to a traumatic event. In one study synthesizing the results of 54 prior studies (Galatzer-Levy, Huang, & Bonanno, 2018) the authors conclude: "Importantly, findings demonstrated that the severity of an event is not a key contributor to [symptoms] . . . .This suggests that psychological and biological factors may have a stronger influence on the development of individual differences in response to stress more than the level of objective severity of an event" (p. 51). In other words, the context of the individual's life, their personal history, their social location and its resulting conditions, and their inner resilience may be more important than the intensity of the event itself in determining its impact. This highlights the importance of protecting the most vulnerable students from PTE exposure and supporting the adolescents who are most at risk for negative outcomes.

However, it's also true that many individuals exposed to such experiences are not, in fact, traumatized: hence the use of the phrase *potentially traumatic experiences*. The majority of people remain healthy and adapt in the face of PTEs. A leading researcher of resilience, George Bonanno (2011) argues that science has focused excessively on psychological symptoms following PTEs and overlooked the majority of people who demonstrate adaptive, resilient outcomes. None of this is to deny in any way the painful reality of posttraumatic stress disorder, depression, or subclinical symptoms that can follow a PTE. It is rather to acknowledge the relative impact of these events and to broaden our understanding of what constitutes trauma.

As we've suggested, two adolescents experiencing the same potentially traumatic event may respond very differently. One might be largely unaffected or recover completely in a very short period. The other might have persistent symptoms of depression, anger, or irritability. What distinguishes these two adolescents? In other words, why are some adolescents more resilient than others? Some personality traits, such as low levels of negative affect, adaptive flexibility, and high perceived self-efficacy have been associated with resilient outcomes. High levels of social support also predict better outcomes after a PTE, as do lower levels of current or past stress. Those demonstrating resilience also tend to think about adversity in a more adaptive way.

Mindfulness as a Component of Treatment for Traumatic Stress

Mindfulness holds particular promise as a component of treatment for traumatic stress. In the hundreds of studies examining mindfulness for a mental health condition, the proportion of the research participants with a trauma history is almost invariably high. So, even when the study is not specifically examining the effects of mindfulness on trauma, we know that trauma has been successfully navigated, given the encouraging results of these studies. What's more, many current trauma treatment approaches feature mindfulness as a key component. The client's capacity for moment-to-moment tracking of sensory experience and acceptance is an essential part of the process of renegotiating and integrating traumatic experiences.

Ortiz and Sibinga (2017), pediatricians and researchers at Johns Hopkins School of Medicine, reviewed the evidence for mindfulness in addressing adverse effects of childhood trauma and toxic stress. Mindfulness has been associated with lower levels of dissociation, healthier coping, and fewer depressive symptoms. They write:

> Mindfulness programs for youth show promise by reducing mood and emotion dysregulation (decrease depressive, self-hostility, PTSD, anxiety and negative affect symptoms), negative-coping with stress, and improved school adaptation (classroom behavior and discipline, social and academic competence), and attention, mitigating negative effects and potential exacerbations of adverse childhood experiences. Mindfulness has also been shown to benefit those important to youth, including parents and teachers. . . . In conclusion, research has

demonstrated that high-quality, structured mindfulness interventions improve mental, behavioral, and physical outcomes in youth. Further, these results in combination with the well-studied interventions in adults suggest promise in preventing the poor health outcomes associated with trauma exposure in childhood. (p. 8)

In their conclusion, they suggest that future research explore the mechanisms of mindfulness and long-term outcomes of mindfulness in trauma survivors and their offspring.

MINDFULNESS, TRAUMA, AND HARM

An important question about mindfulness-based interventions, given the vulnerability of traumatized individuals and the prevalence of trauma among adolescents, is whether they are safe. How much risk is there that mindfulness could precipitate bad effects? Some have suggested that the exuberance surrounding mindfulness has outpaced the data. Though expanding quickly, the science regarding mindfulness is relatively young; important research questions have yet to be answered. Concerned observers have worried that perhaps the mindfulness community has been cavalier about potential harms of the intervention. While we fully agree that the safety of mindfulness should be investigated rather than assumed, there is currently very little evidence of harm and considerable evidence that mindfulness is a low-risk intervention. Much of the data relies on adult samples; more work regarding the safety of the intervention must be done with children and adolescents.

In exploring questions of safety and potential harm, an important factor to consider is *dosage*. There are rigorous mindfulness retreats where adults practice 18 hours a day, in silence, for days, weeks, or months at a time. Clearly, the self-regulatory capacity required for such an experience is different from the capacity required for a 15-minute session offered in a school or a 2-hour weekly class in which students are only practicing mindfulness for several minutes at a time. Though little research has been done on intensive retreats (and still less on retreats geared toward adolescents and young adults), we suspect that the list of cautions or contraindications for intensive retreat practice will be longer than the list of cautions for the low-dose interventions featured in this book. A comprehensive review (Creswell, 2017) of mindfulness interventions published in the *Annual Review of Psychology* concludes that "current evidence-based mindfulness interventions which are offered in smaller spaced doses [than intensive retreats] by trained instructors, carry minimal risks for significant adverse events; furthermore, these mindfulness interventions show the greatest benefits among high trauma/ stress populations" (p. 507). Not only are the vulnerable not harmed by mindfulness, this study suggests, but it appears that they tend to benefit the most from the intervention.

The best available evidence for the presence or absence of harm comes from randomized controlled trials (RCT) that carefully assess adverse events. In a typical trial, participants are randomly assigned to a mindfulness intervention or a *control* group that is assessed in the same ways and at the same interval as the mindfulness group. The researchers are first interested if there are substantially more *adverse events* in one of the groups. Next, the researchers attempt to determine if the adverse event appeared to be directly related to the intervention in question. In one recent review of 36 RCTs that looked at the safety of mindfulness-based interventions (Wong et al., 2018), the authors found that very few adverse effects were related to mindfulness.

A recent article echoes these findings about the relative safety of mindfulness-based programs evidenced by randomized controlled trials. Ruth Baer (2019), an influential mindfulness researcher, provides a number of recommendations for protecting mindfulness-based program participants from harm. While many of the recommendations may not be appropriate given a particular context, we distill or quote the researchers suggestions here to serve as a framework for minimizing risk:

1. Teachers must understand the theoretical and empirical foundations for using the mindfulness-based programs with their population.

2. Identify any conditions that place people at higher risk for difficulties. This list may include adolescents with a history of substance dependence, suicidality, psychosis, severe depression or recent bereavement. However, we should note that mindfulness programs have been adapted for conditions that typically appear on lists of 'exclusion criteria' (PTSD, suicidality, psychosis) and have shown promising results, suggesting that exclusion criteria should be viewed flexibly.

3. Participants should feel invited, rather than pressured, to engage in mindfulness techniques. Clarify the rationale for mindfulness practice.

4. Prevention of harm requires understanding common types of uncomfortable experiences, their usual range of intensity, and distinguishing typical challenges from concerning symptoms.

5. Monitoring for any sustained adverse effects is important. When such events occur, prevention of harm may require adjustments in the participant's practice, discontinuing the program, or referral to other services.

6. The requirement that teachers of mindfulness have their own mindfulness practice may provide further experiential understanding of challenging mind states that will help them work with participants' meditation-related challenges.

Special Cautions

Sometimes, adolescents may be reticent to practice mindfulness initially. They may express concern that they'll be bored or don't like sitting still. It's important to learn to distinguish ordinary resistance from psychological exacerbation. As we describe below, there are warning signs and adaptations that help minimize risk or mitigate harm. **Although more data is needed, there is currently no clear evidence that any particular group of adolescents should be systematically excluded from appropriately "dosed" mindfulness practice with trained instructors because they are at significant risk for harm.**

While teaching mindfulness to a middle school class, Oren noticed one young woman who routinely kept her eyes open during the practices. In private, she shared that she often felt frightened when she closed her eyes and tried to feel her breathing. It reminded her of lying in her bed during an earthquake. Oren modified the instructions for her (encouraging her to keep her eyes open and focus on the sensations of simple hand movements) and referred her to the school mental health counselor for further evaluation and potential treatment for the symptoms associated with the earthquake.

The concern that mindfulness might retraumatize someone is understandable. While specific situations may require modifying the practice, evidence suggests minimal risk for retraumatization. A recent clinical trial of mindfulness for high-risk youth in an urban school district actually found improvements in posttraumatic stress symptoms (Sibinga, Webb, Ghazarian, & Ellen, 2016). None of the 159 students receiving mindfulness experienced any significant negative effects. These data are consistent with clinical trials of mindfulness of adults where even individuals with serious psychiatric conditions derive benefit, practice safely, and stay with the program over time (Khoury et al., 2013a; López-Navarro et al., 2015).

Another possible indicator of treatment-induced negative effects is dropout. When a research participant drops out, it is conceivable they have dropped out because the intervention is not working or because they are experiencing negative effects. Therefore, unusually high dropout rates might serve as a preliminary warning that an intervention could be causing harm. It is thus notable that mindfulness-based interventions have low dropout rates—even lower than the rate in cognitive behavioral therapy (Khoury, Lecomte, Gaudiano & Paquin, 2013b).

We agree that special caution is required in bringing mindfulness to populations at risk for psychiatric distress. We recommend that mindfulness teachers serving such populations work in close collaboration with clinicians or obtain clinical training themselves. We also believe that mindfulness practice is much more likely to *reveal* underlying psychological issues than it is to actually *cause* psychiatric problems. If a brief session of mindfulness precipitates an acute anxiety state or intrusive traumatic memories, we consider this a clear indication of a need for professional mental health evaluation. Continuing mindfulness should be decided in collaboration with a clinician.

That said, concern about harm arising through mindfulness practice can be overestimated because observers may fail to understand how mindfulness works. Practiced for a sufficient period, even beneficial mindfulness practice is virtually certain to precipitate some unpleasant, transient states. However, this doesn't mean that the practice has backfired. Quite the contrary; this is often an indication that practice is unfolding in a productive manner. While mindfulness has soothing effects, it also functions in part as a kind of exposure therapy in which those practicing it are likely to encounter their habits of avoidance. Though such encounters are not pleasant, they represent a genuine therapeutic opportunity rather than a sign that mindfulness practice is causing harm. Competent mindfulness teachers understand this, providing context and support for navigating the challenges.

Mindfulness as Unsystematic Exposure Therapy

Experiential avoidance is defined as an unwillingness to remain in contact with unpleasant thoughts, memories, emotions, and other internal private experiences, even when that avoidance creates additional stress or harm over the long term (Hayes Wilson, Gifford, Follette & Strosahl, 1996). This concept helps explain a broad range of psychological struggles and clinical conditions such as anxiety disorders and depression. Even without a psychiatric condition, most individuals have felt the effects of experiential avoidance in certain situations, which can include procrastination, distraction, suppression, behavioral avoidance, difficulty enduring distress, repression, or denial (Gámez, Chmielewski, Kotov, Ruggero & Watson, 2011).

CONSIDER THIS . . .

Mindfulness is a way of connecting with avoided experience, and in this way, we digest our past.

Although there may be situations when some form of avoidance is adaptive, these are few. Rigid strategies of avoidance and suppression do not appear to be functional in the long run. Suppression has little power to minimize the experience of negative emotion and actually *decreases* the experience of positive emotional experience (Gross & John 2003). Suppressing a specific thought takes mental energy, while the very process of monitoring one's mental space to avoid the thought ironically ensures that it eventually reemerges in consciousness. (Try not thinking about a pink elephant . . .) As Wenzlaff and Wegner (2000) conclude in their definitive review of the subject, "suppression is not simply an ineffective tactic of control; it is counterproductive, helping assure the very state of mind one had hoped to avoid" (p. 83).

Mindfulness practice lies between the extremes of avoidance and entanglement. The former attempts to deal with unwelcome thoughts by cringing, resisting, turning away, or procrastinating. The latter extreme becomes overly fixated on and involved with emotional material. We obsess and ruminate, spinning in endless thoughts that feel urgent. We arrange and rearrange our thoughts as if in so doing we could rearrange the world. We simulate possible futures again and again, strategizing responses to imagined scenarios. Sometimes, these extremes of suppression and entanglement feel like two sides of the same coin: we avoid, then ruminate, and flip back again.

In learning to balance between avoidance and entanglement, what we initially find is not a state of peace but the habitual, gravitational pull of the two extremes. We intend to simply be present and relax, but our mind has other plans. When practitioners discover the push/pull of avoidance and entanglement they often conclude that they're either doing something wrong or that they're not cut out for mindfulness. This is a fundamental misunderstanding of how mindfulness works. The practice isn't about manufacturing happiness; it's about coming to understand and make peace with the things that obstruct happiness. This is a critical distinction to bear in mind. What this means is that the obstacles themselves *are* our path of growth.

To understand how mindfulness affects change and the role these unpleasant experiences play in that process, it can be helpful to draw some parallels between mindfulness practice and exposure therapy. Exposure therapy involves the deliberate introduction of anxiety-provoking stimuli (activities, people, places, internal experiences) with the ultimate goal of changing emotional and behavioral responses to life's experiences. While the usual tendency is to retreat from anxiety-provoking stimuli, individuals move against the tide of avoidance and directly expose themselves to the feared stimulus. Through this exposure, we begin to desensitize to the fear, disprove catastrophic beliefs associated with the fear, and develop new learning. Over time, we form associations between the feared object and the experience of safety.

Typically, exposure therapy is done in a staged way. It begins with some psychoeducation, creating a rationale for the work, building an interpersonal atmosphere of support and care, and learning self-soothing strategies to calm strong emotional responses. The treatment proceeds with a hierarchy of exposures, beginning with a benign encounter with the stimulus and slowly increasing the level of challenge through a series of controlled experiences. At each stage, the individual practices managing their anxiety (the avoidance response), progressing to the next level only after they've gained some mastery and nonavoidance of the stimulus. This process would ideally reduce the avoidant behaviors, create new learning, and restore a sense of well-being.

This approach is sometimes called *systematic* desensitization or systematic exposure therapy. In contrast to this approach, we could say that mindfulness is *unsystematic* exposure therapy. In exposure therapy, the client and therapist formulate a specific plan for exposure; in mindfulness practice, that which we have avoided simply arises on its own, according to its own logic.

In mindfulness, whatever can disturb our peace of mind eventually will. Consider what happens when you sit down to meditate. You're trying to pay attention to your breath and mind your own business, but there it is: anxiety about work or resentment about some situation. As we've mentioned, these unpleasant emotions can feel like a mistake, an intrusion, but they are actually an integral part of the practice. To find balance we need to see directly what disrupts our peace of mind. To understand how our emotional conditioning functions in our lives, we must *experience* that conditioning. When difficult emotions arise, we do what we can to make room for them and find peace with them. When done properly, this practice is quite liberating; we learn little by little how to cease being disturbed by the comings and goings of thoughts, feelings, and sensations. Understanding the nature of this process is essential in guiding adolescents in mindfulness and in particular in discerning between the ordinary, unpleasant parts of the practice and problematic states of distress that could be an indication of deeper psychological needs.

PRODUCTIVE DISCOMFORT VERSUS WORRISOME DISTRESS

This process of making peace with avoided experience is liberating, but it is not pleasant. We could consider it *productive discomfort*. The distress can be related to digesting a particular memory or emotion, or it may be more diffuse. Sometimes the distress is a healthy, productive pain. Here, the teacher provides loving support, normalizes the distress by contextualizing the experience, and offers encouragement to keep going. Other times, the distress may be sufficiently disturbing or intense that it is no longer supportive to continue practicing in the same way. In this case, the instructor would again contextualize the experience and offer encouragement, but they would redirect the student toward a different form of mindfulness practice (or away from the practice temporarily). Distinguishing between these two types of cases is key.

If a student described a challenging experience in meditation practice, there would be a number of considerations on our mind. First, we would consider the individual's overall level of resilience and well-being. Have they been able to complete their work, make friends, and abide by the group agreements? Have they had previous psychological struggles, and if so, how have they been able to manage and integrate those struggles?

Second, we would consider how they are presenting in this moment. How is their behavior right now? Are they jumping from one topic to another, or can they follow the thread of the conversation? In addition to reporting on their verbal output, we'd observe their nonverbal behavior. Does their attention seem steady? Can they hold our gaze, are their eyes darting around, or are they avoiding eye contact entirely? What is the quality of their voice? Are they breathing normally or is their breathing pattern distressed? Does their energy level seem steady or flat, jumpy, and fidgety? How are they responding to our words, presence, and reassurance?

Finally, given all of this information—what we know of their history, the content that they are sharing, and their immediate presentation—we attempt to assess the nature of the distress. Is this the pain of growth or the pain of symptom exacerbation? In either case, does their physical, emotional, verbal, and nonverbal presentation indicate that they are tolerating the distress or struggling too intensely to do so? How responsive is the student to emotional support? When the gentle, kind support of a teacher quickly de-escalates the student, it is less likely to be a cause for concern. This is the most typical situation. Often, students simply need the stability, reassurance, and care of an adult to find their balance.

Exposure therapy entails a bearable dose of one's distress. Eliciting distress that is too intense overwhelms the nervous system and is counterproductive. Consider if the student is reporting a dose of distress that is simply too much for them to handle. If conversation, loving support, and gentle guidance fail to stabilize the student, it may be an indication that there are more significant psychological needs. Depending on your level of training, you might offer further counseling support or refer the student to a clinician for further assessment. Again, we believe that mindfulness is much more likely to reveal psychological impairment rather than to cause it. Regardless, there are cases where formal mindfulness might be stopped and referral for additional psychological support or assessment is most appropriate.

When the distress is a component of healthy psychological growth (rather than a signal of danger), there are some useful adaptations we can make if the student is feeling overwhelmed by their inner experience. These suggestions may be more or less appropriate depending on the context in which you are teaching:

1. Open the eyes and gently gaze, lingering with any visual impression that is positive or has a soothing effect.
2. Do more movement practice, for example, yoga, tai chi, or walking with a focus on natural beauty and the sky.
3. Shorten sitting meditation sessions or practice with eyes open.
4. Deemphasize the exposure aspects of mindfulness practice; feature the soothing aspects more prominently.
5. Emphasize kindness and self-compassion practices.
6. Help them practice mindfulness *out loud*, naming experiences they are having as they practice. This can give the teacher a better under-

standing of their inner life and provide feedback on how they are attending to experience.

7. Have students place a hand on their heart or face and feel the contact points.
8. Have students gently massage or touch a part of their own body, perhaps a very small movement such as rubbing two fingers together, giving attention to pleasant sensations.
9. Help the student track their own level of activation, teaching them to back off whenever they feel out of their comfort zone.
10. Help the student distinguish mindfulness from rumination. Sometimes the line distinguishing these two can be fuzzy, but when mindfulness devolves into pure rumination, it's best to change practices.

A WORD OF CAUTION: MINDFULNESS IS NOT A REPLACEMENT FOR MENTAL HEALTH TREATMENT

As we have seen, mindfulness is playing an increasingly prominent role in mental health treatment. This is a testament to the value of mindfulness practice in improving depression, anxiety, traumatic stress, and a host of associated conditions. We feel enthusiastic about the value of mindfulness-based interventions and also want to note some important cautions for school contexts.

Mental health treatment in schools commonly operates at capacity. Resources are not always available to provide the individualized treatment that might be ideal. Consequently, schools sometimes rely on programming to fill the gaps in mental health care. While mindfulness has value for psychological well-being, the universal group-based delivery of mindfulness practices does *not* constitute a mental health treatment. It is important that schools do not rely on mindfulness, delivered in a low-dose group format, as a replacement for comprehensive mental health treatment.

There are important differences between classroom-based mindfulness programming and mindfulness as a mental health intervention. When mindfulness is employed as a mental health intervention, it is typically delivered by a clinician and incorporates elements of evidence-based mental health treatment. For example, a version of Mindfulness-Based Cognitive Therapy for Children (MBCT-C) borrows heavily from the cognitive-behavioral tradition. MBCT-C includes twelve weekly sessions of 90 minutes, home practice exercises, and other homework assignments. Furthermore, patients might receive other treatment, including individual psychotherapy or psychiatric medication.

Relying heavily on universal classroom-based programming, such as mindfulness, to treat vulnerable students is unwise. Orienting mindfulness lessons in this way places an undue burden on the practice and can undercut the central element of curiosity and exploration. It is unfortunate when teachers find themselves bending the practices to meet needs that the curriculum was not intended to meet. This will tend to compromise the joy and connection that can arise when mindfulness is offered without rigid agendas and without unrealistic hopes of healing students who need more focused mental health attention.

CHAPTER 10

Our Moment:
Expanding the Circle of Care

Across evolutionary time, our species has inherited some beautiful traits. Foremost among these qualities are empathy, compassion, and the urge to help others. When we look inward, we find a natural responsiveness to the suffering of others. When we listen deeply to the calling in our own hearts, we tend to hold others with care, challenge injustice, and live generously. When our own mind is clear and our heart open, the natural response is to look around for ways to help others and engage with the world in a meaningful way. As we take care of our own emotional needs, energy is freed up to attend to the needs of others.

Though mindfulness doesn't attempt to provide a comprehensive ethical framework, it isn't ethically neutral. As the philosopher Peter Singer argues, "Ethics is inescapable." We can't teach mindfulness without implicitly supporting certain values. Mindfulness practice is guided by values for kindness, generosity, empathy, and sensitivity to harm, all which are often enhanced as outcomes. The quality of attention generated in mindfulness can be described as *nonviolent*. We are learning to be aware of thoughts, feelings, and sensations in a patient, tolerant way. We practice nonaggression inwardly. As we invest kindness, so we grow in kindness moment by moment. Indeed, it's not surprising that mindfulness practice catalyzes the motivation to benefit others (Berry et al., 2018). When we experience the poignancy of our own suffering, we hear the cries of the world more clearly. As adolescents learn to stand more fully in their own shoes, the capacity to stand in someone else's shoes grows.

Sometimes, mindfulness is criticized for being a form of self-absorption or a practice for privileged people to feel more comfortable with the ennui of their bourgeois lifestyle. There is a risk that mindfulness can be co-opted by consumerism, individualism, and indulgence and that it can be misappropriated as a tool to deaden rather than enliven our moral commitments. While the ethical North Star of mindfulness practice is nonharming and ethical sensitivity, this can be eroded as the practice is inevitably affected by our current cultural, social, political, and economic context.

Yet, critiques of mindfulness as a tool of neoliberal capitalism often fail to attend to the importance of context in how mindfulness tools are shared and practiced. Mindfulness, for example, ought not be used to soothe the anxiety of fossil fuel company executives dealing with the strain of environmental protests. Nevertheless, the need to await some utopian vision in order to implement mindfulness within problematic institutions is short-sighted. In schools, for example, mindfulness is often a lifeline for finding alternatives to unhealthy coping mechanisms and developing more resilience. While this doesn't solve issues of wealth inequality or systemic oppression, it gives those suffering under its weight a chance to heal and breathe enough to mobilize for change. Many of the stories we hear from educators, and that we ourselves receive as teachers, indicate that people from historically marginalized communities often stand to benefit the most from the healing potential of mindfulness. When you directly witness the gratitude that people feel for these practices, it is difficult to adhere to abstract rationales for withholding such practices.

It is easy to equate mindfulness practice with passivity when it is not situated within a framework of ethical responsibility. After all, most formal mindfulness exercises entail sitting still with eyes closed, face expressionless, the attention turned inwards. Yet the whole trajectory of the practice, when engaged sincerely, brings us into deeper contact with the effects of our actions as they ripple outward, with the interdependence of life. The inward turn of mindfulness is actually an attempt to become *less entangled* with the ups and downs of our personal lives. As we grow more comfortable in our own skin and less preoccupied with our emotional life, as we become less dependent on arranging conditions to meet our preferences, our attention naturally turns toward others. As we encounter the poignancy of our own vulnerability and see the functioning of our own mind and body more clearly, we cannot help but grow in compassion for others.

As educators, a central part of our vocation is to inspire and empower youth to think for themselves. We are tasked with providing some orientation around the value of nonharming, while encouraging students to discover for themselves their own expression of their ethical values. For example, Khalila Gillett Archer of iBme explains that the aim of teen retreats is to provide tools for kids to more deeply understand themselves so they have more freedom around their actions and choices. "It's about helping young people to get in touch with their own values and purpose more deeply, and giving them skills to act in the world rather than being controlled by their conditioning, by others, or by outside forces."

As we've explored, mindfulness practice is about much more than attentional training or behavior modification. Mindfulness helps adolescents identify their own values. It's a form of deep inner listening. As author and spiritual teacher Ram Dass once said, "The quieter you become, the more you can hear." We view this as a critically important element of our work with adolescents: we support them to understand what they care about most and to align their behavior with their values. In the practice, we are not merely relinquishing the urges to act out unhelpful habits; we are also learning to discern our own moral commitments. As educators, we can validate this movement of our students' hearts.

The practice of mindfulness is meant to empower people. It transforms life from a labyrinth of accumulation, control, and acquisition into a path of learning. We move out of the mode of constantly seeking something to fulfill us and into a mode in which each experience is an invitation to grow. Cultivating awareness gives us the capacity to see more clearly. As awareness grows, we apply that clarity to our lives—personally and collectively. Without this awareness, we are likely to act unconsciously out of habit, fear, or self-centeredness.

This kind of independent, courageous awareness needs to be fostered. When you teach, support your students to connect the radical exploration of their inner life with a critical questioning of the structures of the world in which we live. One of the deep lessons of mindfulness practice is that the stories, assumptions, metaphors, and frameworks that have ordered our lives are without ultimate justification. What seemed utterly natural and necessary is in fact contingent, a product of many conditions. It is not to be obeyed blindly. This opens a space for a radical interrogation. Engage them in conversation about the world they'd like to create. How might things look differently? How can you empower them today to take steps in that direction?

We view mindfulness practice as a tool for training moral leaders. Increasingly, we see youth taking moral leadership in our culture. Youth are often at the vanguard of social change movements. They tend to be more suspicious of traditional authority, more willing to rebel, and less encumbered by outmoded ethical standards. (Perhaps you yourself spent time on high school or college campuses attending rallies and sit-ins, defying outdated thinking and pushing the edges for change!) We rely on youth to challenge the ethical status quo. After 17 people were killed in 2018 at Majory Stoneman Douglas High School in Florida, a network of surviving students emerged to fiercely, and very publicly, advocate for measures counteracting gun violence. The March for Our Lives, a student-led event attracting more than a million people, was one of the largest public demonstrations in our nation's history. The public displays of grief, strength, and moral clarity have influenced the tenor of the national debate and mobilized civic participation among young voters. Emma Gonzalez's impassioned, personal speech did more for the hearts of this country than any congressperson could have on television. She asked folks to stand with her and cry together (Amatulli, 2018).

CONSIDER THIS . . .

Hold a Council Circle asking the question: What are your strengths and how can you use them for the betterment of those around you? Often kids don't think they're good enough at anything, but what if they only had to be good at one thing? To serve well, we need a diversity of skills and minds.

One of the organizing principles in this work is that we can, indeed should, be learning from our young people. Listening to the moral concerns of adolescents can change our own sense of moral responsibility. Observing their energy, creativity, and grit can remind us of our own potential for good and our ethical commitments. When you practice, notice when and how habitual ways of relating to yourself, others, or issues of social change and transformation in the world creep in. Where do feelings of fear, despair, or helplessness arise? Can you make space for that experience and then listen more closely for the beliefs or fixed views that are feeding those emotions? Can you return to the moment with a fresh perspective and an open heart? Can you continually let go of ingrained ways of thinking and being and meet this moment as an unknown mystery? Recall your students and allow their brightness to inspire you.

Adolescents regularly express their fear that adults have abdicated their role to protect future generations. This is perhaps most evident in the realm of climate activism. At 15 years of age, Greta Thunberg's pleas to ensure the viability of the world for future generations garnered international recognition. She was subsequently nominated for the Nobel Peace Prize by the Norwegian Parliament. At the international summit in Davos, her speech (Thunberg, 2019) included this stark appeal:

> We are facing a disaster of unspoken sufferings for enormous amounts of people. And now is not the time for speaking politely or focusing on what we can or cannot say. Now is the time to speak clearly . . . Adults keep saying: "We owe it to the young people to give them hope." But I don't want your hope. I don't want you to be hopeful. I want you to

panic. I want you to feel the fear I feel every day. And then I want you to act. I want you to act as you would in a crisis. I want you to act as if our house is on fire. Because it is.

Our species is failing to fully appreciate that our ecological destructiveness will have shattering effects for current and subsequent generations. Throughout this book, we've celebrated the value of empathy. But empathy can be distorted by space and time. We are more empathetic to the suffering near us even though our ethical commitments apply regardless of whether a person is in our neighborhood or on a different continent. Further, the moral importance of outcomes in the future is discounted, sometimes dismissed entirely. It's time to wise up. Youth recognize that they are inheriting the legacy of our negligence. How can we learn from their courage, support their voices, and join in partnership with their demands? Mindfulness practice provides one small piece of this puzzle.

The practice can support this work in several ways. As we've mentioned, the core cultivation of clear, balanced awareness strengthens moral discernment and critical thinking. The strengthening of positive states like kindness, empathy, generosity, and so forth supports resilience in facing the challenges of our times. On a deeper level, as the practice unfolds, we begin to see how the forces of ignorance, greed, self-centeredness, and hostility that are devastating the planet function on a moment-to-moment level in our minds. Connecting the microcosm of our own mind to the functioning of our community, society, and world will be necessary for our ethical evolution.

REMEMBERING OUR PAST AND UNDERSTANDING SOCIAL IDENTITY

As philosopher George Santayana once famously said, "Those who cannot remember the past are condemned to repeat it." What we cannot experience consciously will distort our behavior. At the collective level, forgetting is dangerous. Societies remember and forget in distinctive patterns; out of these selective memories, we create myths and a sense of national identity. Many of the most painful legacies of our history are selectively elided: the founding violence against Native Americans, the horror of slavery, the succession of institutionalized advantages for select groups, the rapacious extraction of natural resources. As a consequence, our national self-image is incomplete and fragile. As we remember more of the pain of our history, we can examine the legacies that create our current moment. Increasingly, students are becoming conscious of the structural conditions creating suffering: systemic factors in the education system, poverty, institutional racism, community violence. Teens often yearn to discuss these issues in a real way: "Why does my neighborhood look like this? How come there are more liquor stores than supermarkets? Why do some kids have so much and others so little?"

These conversations are not easy and can elicit defensiveness in some adults. One teacher we've previously discussed, Morris Ervin, tells the story of leading an assembly on mindfulness at one inner city school, where he asked an auditorium of nearly 1000 kids: "Raise your hand if you've ever had a parent who was incarcerated. Raise your hand if you've ever been affected by domestic violence. If you've ever experienced police brutality?" A sea of hands went up with each question, and the teens were riveted. Here was someone finally telling the truth about their lives. He had their undivided attention because he spoke to their experience. Yet the faculty and administrative staff—who were mostly middle-class white folks—thought he was bashing the police. They didn't fully appreciate the emotional gravity of those sociological truths, nor Morris's intentions in pointing out the reality of the pain in their lives. We have seen how it is possible to point to these realities with the intention of healing and to engage kids in meaningful conversations that help them step into positions of leadership in their schools and communities.

Woven throughout this work with young people are the ways in which our own social location and identity interface with that of our students. In order to be most effective with teens, it's important to guard against perpetuating the dynamics of oppression around race, class, gender, sexuality, ability, or heteronormative expectations.

Understanding these ways that bias and power dynamics have informed our perspectives is vital in reaching across lines of difference. Reflecting on the distinctive character of our experience—especially the experience of privilege—sensitizes us to ways we might fail empathically. For example, some studies have shown how white teachers are more inclined to interpret behaviors of students of color as disrespectful or problematic than those of white students. Similarly, students of color often face more frequent and harsher disciplinary actions than white students (Skiba et al., 2011). These kinds of biases are damaging to our students personally, perpetuate long-standing social systems, and interfere with our ability to realize our deeper intentions in our work.

Your own practice is an indispensable asset here. To practice mindfulness is to know the mind directly and uncover its biases. Remember, mindfulness itself is the process of paying attention in a balanced and equanimous way. Developing this quality of awareness entails recognizing when the mind is unbalanced or charged with grasping or aversion—when it is biased for or against something.

In this practice, we quickly realize that we are not neutral observers. The author Robert Heinlein (1953) remarked that we humans are not so much rational animals, but *rationalizing* animals. Acknowledging this, we can begin to tease apart the ways in which our minds lean toward or away from certain experiences, situations, or people. We see this when resisting an unpleasant sensation, avoiding someone, or discounting their ideas because of their political views, race, gender, or any other attribute. Sometimes, bias is signaled by a sense of tension. It takes humility to look honestly at our biases.

As we practice, we discover successively deeper layers of preference and bias. Encountering these patterns, we can begin to observe their operation in real time. We learn how such attitudes arise from automatic associations in our memory based on past experience and social conditioning. Once we become more aware of a particular mental habit, it holds less sway over our actions. Once we notice a tendency to lean in one direction, we might consciously choose a new response. Each time we become cognizant of a previously unconscious bias, our world expands.

At first, this process can be difficult or surprising. Over time, we become more tolerant to this process of uncovering ignorance. With each new awareness or shift in perspective, our humility deepens. Instead of needing to have things figured out or believing we must achieve some ideal state of perfection, we learn to rest in the deep humility of *not knowing*. This kind of openness fosters deep curiosity and creates fertile ground for learning and development.

Some of this work can be done on our own, but we can never achieve a "God's-eye view" of ourselves, to use a phrase from the philosopher, Hilary Putnam. We rely on others to help fill out our self-understanding. The process of unlearning bias is supported by resources like antiracism and antioppression trainings and books. Take time to reflect on your own social identities. Are you able to see and understand things from multiple perspectives, particularly the perspective of those who experience different degrees of access to social power and privilege?

Practice being open to feedback from students, colleagues, and supervisors. We can treat our lives like an open feedback loop. The defensiveness that feedback can elicit highlights the architecture of our ego. We fight to maintain our view of ourselves in the face of ego-challenging information. This is such a natural response. Still, we can become more curious about the nature of our defensiveness rather than avoiding a sober view of ourselves. This process takes a lot of tenderness. Importantly, what we're describing can be liberating regardless of the accuracy of the feedback. We usually think that we accept accurate feedback and refuse inaccurate feedback. In some sense, that's right, but our reaction to feedback (accurate or inaccurate) always contains some wisdom about how we define ourselves and the pressure points in our own egos. As our self-definition becomes more fluid, we can engage with others in more potent, relaxed, intimate, and nourishing ways.

SUFFERING IS AN INTERDISCIPLINARY PROBLEM

As we've mentioned at various points, mindfulness has its limits. It is not enough to resolve broad, societal challenges (nor was it intended to be). It's important not to give the impression that if you're mindful, your problems will disappear. Mindfulness provides a way of opening to and holding the pain in life, healing the past and building resilience, but it's insufficient to address the concrete challenges we face. Suffering is an *interdisciplinary* problem. Progress will reflect sophisticated efforts to understand the causal processes that produce suffering (personally and collectively) and will draw on wisdom from many traditions: medicine, science, philosophy, history, art, religion. If we try to employ mindfulness to treat every ill, we undermine the seriousness of the suffering and simultaneously diminish the potency of mindfulness. When we practice mindfulness with an urgent demand that it resolve some particular problem, the patient, exploratory spirit of the practice is lost, and with that, much of its goodness evaporates.

> **CONSIDER THIS . . .**
> *Suffering is an interdisciplinary problem. Matching medicine and disease is important. Respecting the limits of mindfulness actually honors the practice, rather than disrespecting it.*

While we're cautious about the scope of mindfulness, it is not a form of passivity, as we emphasized earlier. When people hear the meditation instruction to allow experience to be just as it is (aimed at strengthening the nonreactive, equanimous aspect of mindfulness), this is interpreted as a global recommendation for passive nonengagement in the world. Equanimity is about accepting our sensory and mental experience in this moment: feelings, thoughts, sensations. All of this can be affirmed, accepted, known with awareness, and met with an open heart. That said, mindfulness is not about accepting all external situations: we very well may need to act to change and improve a situation. There are dangerous situations, both personally and collectively, that would be harmful to accept or allow to remain just as they are. Your own wisdom determines which situations need change and which can be accepted. Importantly, acceptance of our inner experience need not be in conflict with making changes in the world.

THE WISE COUNSEL OF OUR OWN MORTALITY

Peter Singer (2011) describes moral progress as an expanding circle of moral concern. Evolutionarily, we are conditioned to care for and protect our own family or tribe. But the human heart can hold much more. The scope of care grows to include broader groups, an entire country, a family of countries, all humans, all living creatures, and even the world itself. What catalyzes this expansion in our circle of concern? How we can develop this kind of inclusivity in our heart as a way of modeling that potential for our students?

Each of us may find our own way to transform the boundaries we draw around our heart. For some, increasing the understanding of how all life is interconnected moves us in this direction. For others, reflecting on our shared human longing for happiness and fulfillment can break down barriers. The formal practice of loving-kindness meditation is designed to work in a similar way, sending wishes to progressively more challenging persons and all-encompassing groups in order to expand the circle of care from its narrow confines.

There is another powerful method that we wish to offer as a way of supporting you to find strength, resilience, and an ever widening heart in your work with adolescents and young people. Although perhaps counterintuitive, the contemplation of our own death can be cause for deepened moral concern and a wider circle of care. We might imagine that thoughts about death might harden or close the heart. Yet as anyone who has experienced the loss of a loved one knows, alongside the grief, facing the reality of mortality heightens the poignancy and appreciation of life. Writer Amy Krouse Rosenthal (2005), who subsequently died of cancer, shared this:

> When I am feeling dreary, annoyed, and generally unimpressed by life, I imagine what it would be like to come back to this world for just a day after having been dead. I imagine how sentimental I would feel about the very things I once found stupid, hateful, or mundane. Oh, there's a light switch! I haven't seen a light switch in so long! I didn't realize how much I missed light switches! Oh! Oh! And look—the stairs up to our front porch are still completely cracked! Hello cracks! Let me get a good look at you. And there's my neighbor, standing there, fantastically alive, just the same, still punctuating her sentences with "you know what I'm saying?" Why did that bother me? It's so . . . endearing.

What does the thought of mortality do to your own mind and heart? Initially, there may be a wave of fear or emotional contraction, but if we can weather that preliminary shudder of emotion, other sentiments can emerge. As the poet Mary Oliver (1992) wrote, "I don't want to end up simply having visited this world."

Awareness of impermanence enhances the vibrancy of life and invites us to appreciate the beauty and goodness that is already here. We can get so accustomed to the ordinary acts of kindness, care, and goodness that surround us every day that we overlook them. Pain and problems command our attention; we forget our good fortune. Remembering that we won't have that goodness forever reawakens the preciousness of our life and cuts through the pettiness that might otherwise preoccupy our attention. It's also an essential factor to sustain our teaching. We've spoken at various points about the immense challenges educators face today. Perhaps you work with young people who are surrounded by challenging conditions. Perhaps you sometimes feel like Sisyphus, working for change and healing in impossible conditions, against the odds. Attending to the moments of goodness in your own life, and helping your kids to find and appreciate them in theirs, is another way our mindfulness practice can play a role in the healing of our world.

This recognition of our own fragility recalls another existential truth: though we influence much, we're ultimately not in control; we do not govern the tides of pleasure and pain. In the end, we leave everything behind, but for our legacy of care. In an article, "When Things Go Missing," *The New Yorker* essayist Kathryn Schulz reflects on the death of her father and the importance of relinquishing the need to hold life still:

It is breathtaking, the extinguishing of consciousness. Yet that loss, too— our own ultimate unbeing—is dwarfed by the grander scheme. When we are experiencing it, loss often feels like an anomaly, a disruption in the usual order of things. In fact, though, it is the usual order of things. Entropy, mortality, extinction: the entire plan of the universe consists of losing, and life amounts to a reverse savings account in which we are eventually robbed of everything. Our dreams and plans and jobs and knees and backs and memories, the childhood friend, the husband of fifty years, the father of forever, the keys to the house, the keys to the car, the keys to the kingdom, the kingdom itself: sooner or later, all of it drifts into the Valley of Lost Things. There's precious little solace for this, and zero redress; we will lose everything we love in the end. But why should that matter so much? By definition, we do not live in the end: we live all along the way . . . No matter what goes missing, the wallet or the father, the lessons are the same. Disappearance reminds us to notice, transience to cherish, fragility to defend. Loss is a kind of external conscience, urging us to make better use of our finite days. As Whitman knew, our brief crossing is best spent attending to all that we see: honoring what we find noble, denouncing what we cannot abide, recognizing that we are inseparably connected to all of it, including what is not yet upon us, including what is already gone. We are here to keep watch, not to keep (2017).

If there were a phrase to encapsulate mindfulness practice, it might be something like "we are here to keep watch, not to keep." If they are fortunate, our kids need not yet feel the full weight of finitude. We hold this truth for them. With our understanding, we open to transience in a way that unbinds our heart and frees us to live a life of service.

REFERENCES

Adolescence research must grow up. (2018, February 21). Retrieved from https://www.nature.com/articles/d41586-018-02185-w

Amatulli, J. (2018, March 24). Emma Gonzalez stands on stage in total silence to remember Parkland shooting. Retrieved from https://www.huffpost.com/entry/emma-gonzalez-spends-6-minutes-20-seconds-in-silence-to-remember-shooting_n_5ab69b82e4b0decad04a7a32

American Psychiatric Association. (1980). *Diagnostic and statistical manual of mental disorders* (3rd ed.). Washington, DC: Author.

Arnett, J. J. (1999). Adolescent storm and stress, reconsidered. *American Psychologist, 54*(5), 317–326.

Baer, R., Crane, C., Miller, E., & Kuyken, W. (in press). Doing no harm in mindfulness-based programs: Conceptual issues and empirical findings. *Clinical Psychology Review.*

Barlow, D. H., Farchione, T. J., Fairholme, C. P., Ellard, K. K., Boisseau, C. L., Allen, L. B., & May, J. T. E. (2010). *Unified protocol for transdiagnostic treatment of emotional disorders: Therapist guide.* New York: Oxford University Press.

Berry, D. R., Cairo, A. H., Goodman, R. J., Quaglia, J. T., Green, J. D., & Brown, K. W. (2018). Mindfulness increases prosocial responses toward ostracized strangers through empathic concern. *Journal of Experimental Psychology: General, 147*(1), 93–112.

Bissanti, M., Brown, D. P., Pasari, J. (in press). The development and training of attention skills in children and adolescents.

Bonanno, G. A., Westphal, M., & Mancini, A. D. (2011). Resilience to loss and potential trauma. *Annual Review of Clinical Psychology, 7,* 511–535.

Bowlby, J. (1969/2008). *Attachment*. New York: Basic Books.

Bradley, R., Greene, J., Russ, E., Dutra, L., & Westen, D. (2005). A multidimensional meta-analysis of psychotherapy for PTSD. *American Journal of Psychiatry, 162*(2), 214–227.

Brensilver, M. (2016). "The secular qualities of mindfulness." Retrieved from https://www.mindfulschools.org/foundational-concepts/mindfulness-and-secularity/

Brown, Daniel P., & Elliot, David S. (2016). *Attachment disturbances in adults: Treatment for comprehensive repair.* New York: Norton.

Brown, K. W., & Ryan, R. M. (2003). The benefits of being present: Mindfulness and its role in psychological well-being. *Journal of Personality and Social Psychology, 84*(4), 822.

Bryan, C. J., Yeager, D. S., Hinojosa, C. P., Chabot, A., Bergen, H., Kawamura, M., & Steubing, F. (2016). Harnessing adolescent values to motivate healthier eating. *Proceedings of the National Academy of Sciences, 113*(39), 10830–10835.

Copeland, W. E., Keeler, G., Angold, A., & Costello, E. J. (2007). Traumatic events and posttraumatic stress in childhood. *Archives of General Psychiatry, 64*(5), 577–584.

Creswell, J. D. (2017). Mindfulness interventions. *Annual Review of Psychology, 68*, 491–516.

Dahl, C. J., Lutz, A., & Davidson, R. J. (2015). Reconstructing and deconstructing the self: Cognitive mechanisms in meditation practice. *Trends in Cognitive Sciences, 19*(9), 515–523.

Dahl, R. E., Allen, N. B., Wilbrecht, L., & Suleiman, A. B. (2018). Importance of investing in adolescence from a developmental science perspective. *Nature, 554*(7693), 441–450.

Dahl, R. E. (2004). Adolescent brain development: A period of vulnerabilities and opportunities. *Annals of the New York Academy of Sciences, 1021*(1), 1–22.

Dalai Lama. (2009). *The art of happiness: A handbook for living.* New York: Penguin.

Davidson, R. J., & Begley, S. (2012). *The emotional life of your brain: How its unique patterns affect the way you think, feel, and live—and how you can change them.* Hudson Street Press.

Degenhardt, L., Stockings, E., Patton, G., Hall, W. D., & Lynskey, M. (2016). The increasing global health priority of substance use in young people. *The Lancet Psychiatry, 3*(3), 251–264.

Desbordes, G., Gard, T., Hoge, E. A., Hölzel, B. K., Kerr, C., Lazar, S. W., . . . & Vago, D. R. (2015). Moving beyond mindfulness: defining equanimity as an outcome measure in meditation and contemplative research. *Mindfulness, 6*(2), 356–372.

Duncan, L. E., Ratanatharathorn, A., Aiello, A. E., Almli, L. M., Amstadter, A. B., Ashley-Koch, A. E., . . . Bradley, B. (2018). Largest GWAS of PTSD yields genetic overlap with schizophrenia and sex differences in heritability. *Molecular Psychiatry, 23*(3), 666–673.

Durlak, J. A., Weissberg, R. P., Dymnicki, A. B., Taylor, R. D., & Schellinger, K. B. (2011). The impact of enhancing students' social and emotional learning: A meta-analysis of school-based universal interventions. *Child Development, 82*(1), 405–432.

Erikson, E. (1968). *Identity: Youth and crisis.* New York: Norton.

Felitti, V. J., Anda, R. F., Nordenberg, D., Williamson, D. F., Apitz, A. M., Edwards, et al. (1998). Relationship of childhood abuse and household dysfunction to many of the leading causes of death in adults. *American Journal of Preventive Medicine, 14*(4), 245–258.

Forbes, S., & Fikretoglu, D. (2018). Building resilience: The conceptual basis and research evidence for resilience training programs. *Review of General Psychology, 22*(4), 452–468.

Fox, J., & Moreland, J. J. (2015). The dark side of social networking sites: An exploration of the relational and psychological stressors associated with Facebook use and affordances. *Computers in Human Behavior, 45*, 168–176.

Galatzer-Levy, I. R., Huang, S. H., & Bonanno, G. A. (2018). Trajectories of resilience and dysfunction following potential trauma: A review and statistical evaluation. *Clinical Psychology Review, 63*, 41–55.

Gámez, W., Chmielewski, M., Kotov, R., Ruggero, C., & Watson, D. (2011). Development of a measure of experiential avoidance: The Multidimensional Experiential Avoidance Questionnaire. *Psychological Assessment, 23*(3), 692–713.

Gendlin, Eugene. (1981). *Focusing.* New York: Bantam.

Gilbert, P., & Procter, S. (2006). Compassionate mind training for people with high shame and self-criticism: Overview and pilot study of a group therapy approach. *Clinical Psychology & Psychotherapy: An International Journal of Theory & Practice, 13*(6), 353–379.

Goyal, M., Singh, S., Sibinga, E. M., Gould, N. F., Rowland-Seymour, A., Sharma, R., . . . & Ranasinghe, P. D. (2014). Meditation programs for psychological stress and well-being: A systematic review and meta-analysis. *JAMA Internal Medicine, 174*(3), 357–368.

Gross, J. J., & John, O. P. (2003). Individual differences in two emotion regulation processes: Implications for affect, relationships, and well-being. *Journal of Personality and Social Psychology, 85*(2), 348–362.

Haker, K., Kawohl, W., Herwig, U., & Rössler, W. (2013). Mirror neuron activity during contagious yawning—An fMRI study. *Brain Imaging and Behavior, 7*(1), 28–34.

Hanh, T. N. (2002). *Anger: Wisdom for Cooling the Flames.* New York: Penguin.

Hanson, Rick. (2018). *Resilient: How to grow an unshakable core of calm, strength, and happiness.* New York: Harmony.

Haslam, N. (2016). Concept creep: Psychology's expanding concepts of harm and pathology. *Psychological Inquiry, 27*(1), 1–17.

Hayes, S. C., Wilson, K. G., Gifford, E. V., Follette, V. M., & Strosahl, K. (1996). Experiential avoidance and behavioral disorders: A functional dimensional approach to diagnosis and treatment. *Journal of Consulting and Clinical Psychology, 64*(6), 1152–1168.

Heinlein, R. A. (1953). "Gulf,". *Assignment in Eternity. New York: New American Library.*

Himelstein, S. (2013). *A mindfulness-based approach for working with high-risk adolescents.* New York: Routledge.

Himelstein, S. (2018). Three tips for working with resistant teens. Retrieved from https://centerforadolescentstudies.com/3-tips-for-working-with-resistant-teens/

Iacoboni, M., & Lehrer, J. (2008). The mirror neuron revolution: Explaining what makes humans social. *Scientific American.* Retrieved from https://www.scientificamerican.com/article/the-mirror-neuron-revolut/

Jaacks, L. M., Vandevijvere, S., Pan, A., McGowan, C. J., Wallace, C., Imamura, F., . . . Ezzati, M. (2019). The obesity transition: Stages of the global epidemic. *The Lancet Diabetes & Endocrinology, 7*(3), 231–240.

Jennings, P. A. (2018). *The trauma-sensitive classroom: Building resilience with compassionate teaching.* New York: Norton.

Johnston, L. D., Miech, R. A., O'Malley, P. M., Bachman, J. G., Schulenberg, J. E., & Patrick, M. E. (2019). *Monitoring the Future national survey results on drug use 1975–2018: Overview, key findings on adolescent drug use.* Ann Arbor: Institute for Social Research, University of Michigan.

Kabat-Zinn, J. (2003). Mindfulness-based interventions in context: Past, present, and future. *Clinical psychology: Science and Practice, 10*(2), 144–156.

Kessler, R. C., Coccaro, E. F., Fava, M., Jaeger, S., Jin, R., & Walters, E. (2006). The prevalence and correlates of DSM-IV intermittent explosive disorder in the National Comorbidity Survey Replication. *Archives of General Psychiatry, 63*(6), 669–678.

Khoury, B., Lecomte, T., Fortin, G., Masse, M., Therien, P., Bouchard, V., . . . & Hofmann, S. G. (2013a). Mindfulness-based therapy: A comprehensive meta-analysis. *Clinical Psychology Review, 33*, 763–771.

Khoury, B., Lecomte, T., Gaudiano, B. A., & Paquin, K. (2013b). Mindfulness interventions for psychosis: A meta-analysis. *Schizophrenia Research*, *150*(1), 176–184.

Klingbeil, D. A., Renshaw, T. L., Willenbrink, J. B., Copek, R. A., Chan, K. T., Haddock, A., . . . Clifton, J. (2017). Mindfulness-based interventions with youth: A comprehensive meta-analysis of group-design studies. *Journal of School Psychology*, *63*, 77–103.

Kross, E., Verduyn, P., Demiralp, E., Park, J., Lee, D. S., Lin, N., . . . & Ybarra, O. (2013). Facebook use predicts declines in subjective well-being in young adults. *PloS One*, *8*(8), e69841.

Kuyken, W., Warren, F. C., Taylor, R. S., Whalley, B., Crane, C., Bondolfi, G., . . . Segal, Z. (2016). Efficacy of mindfulness-based cognitive therapy in prevention of depressive relapse: An individual patient data meta-analysis from randomized trials. *JAMA Psychiatry*, *73*(6), 565–574.

Lakoff, G., & Johnson, M. (2008). *Metaphors we live by.* Chicago: University of Chicago Press.

Leary, M. R., Tate, E. B., Adams, C. E., Batts Allen, A., & Hancock, J. (2007). Self-compassion and reactions to unpleasant self-relevant events: The implications of treating oneself kindly. *Journal of Personality and Social Psychology*, *92*(5), 887–904.

López-Navarro, E., Del Canto, C., Belber, M., Mayol, A., Fernández-Alonso, O., Lluis, J., . . . & Chadwick, P. (2015). Mindfulness improves psychological quality of life in community-based patients with severe mental health problems: A pilot randomized clinical trial. *Schizophrenia Research*, *168*(1–2), 530–536.

Ludwig, D. S., & Kabat-Zinn, J. (2008). Mindfulness in medicine. *Journal of the American Medical Association*, *300*(11), 1350–1352.

Marsh, I. C., Chan, S. W. Y., & MacBeth, A. (2018). Self-compassion and psychological distress in adolescents—A meta-analysis. *Mindfulness*, *9*(4), 1011–1027.

McKenna, C. (2015). Getting "buy-in" in middle & high school mindfulness teaching. Presented at Bridging Hearts and Minds Conference. University of California San Diego, San Diego, California.

McLaughlin, K. A., Koenen, K. C., Hill, E. D., Petukhova, M., Sampson, N. A., Zaslavsky, A. M., & Kessler, R. C. (2013). Trauma exposure and post-traumatic stress disorder in a national sample of adolescents. *Journal of the American Academy of Child & Adolescent Psychiatry, 52*(8), 815–830.

Mindful Schools (2018). *"The Role of the Mindfulness Teacher,"* Mindful Educator Essentials Module Notes, Week 2, page 4.

Montgomery, A. (2013). *Neurobiology essentials for clinicians: What every therapist needs to know.* New York: Norton.

Mrazek, M. D., Franklin, M. S., Phillips, D. T., Baird, B., & Schooler, J. W. (2013). Mindfulness training improves working memory capacity and GRE performance while reducing mind wandering. *Psychological Science 24*(5),776–781.

Neff, K. D., & McGehee, P. (2010). Self-compassion and psychological resilience among adolescents and young adults. *Self and Identity, 9*(3), 225–240.

Neff, K. D., & Vonk, R. (2009). Self-compassion versus global self-esteem: Two different ways of relating to oneself. *Journal of Personality, 77*(1), 23–50.

Neff, K. D. (2003). Development and validation of a scale to measure self-compassion. *Self and Identity, 2*(3), 223–250.

Nussbaum, M. (2002). In Harmon, J. L. (Ed.). *Take my advice: Letters to the next generation from people who know a thing or two.* New York: Simon and Schuster.

Oliver, M. (1992). *New and selected poems, volume one.* Boston: Beacon Press.

Ortiz, R., & Sibinga, E. (2017). The role of mindfulness in reducing the adverse effects of childhood stress and trauma. *Children, 4*(3), 1–19,

Palmer, Parker J. (2007) *The courage to teach.* San Francisco: Jossey-Bass.

Patton, G. C., Sawyer, S. M., Santelli, J. S., Ross, D. A., Afifi, R., Allen, N. B., . . . Kakuma, R. (2016). Our future: a Lancet commission on adolescent health and wellbeing. *The Lancet, 387*(10036), 2423–2478.

Polusny, M. A., Erbes, C. R., Thuras, P., Moran, A., Lamberty, G. J., Collins, R. C., . . . & Lim, K. O. (2015). Mindfulness-based stress reduction for posttraumatic stress disorder among veterans: A randomized clinical trial. *Journal of the American Medical Association, 314*(5), 456–465.

Porges, S. (2011). *Polyvagal theory.* New York: Norton.

Randall, J. G., Oswald, F. L., & Beier, M. E. (2014). Mind-wandering, cognition, and performance: A theory-driven meta-analysis of attention regulation. *Psychological Bulletin, 140*(6), 1411–1431.

Roeser, R. W., Schonert-Reichl, K. A., Jha, A., Cullen, M., Wallace, L., Wilensky, R., . . . Harrison, J. (2013). Mindfulness training and reductions in teacher stress and burnout: Results from two randomized, waitlist-control field trials. *Journal of Educational Psychology, 105*(3), 787–804.

Roeser, R. W., Skinner, E., Beers, J., & Jennings, P. A. (2012). Mindfulness training and teachers' professional development: An emerging area of research and practice. *Child Development Perspectives, 6*(2), 167–173.

Rogers, Fred. (1995). *You are special: Words of wisdom for all ages from a beloved neighbor.* New York: Penguin.

Rosenthal, A. K. (2005). *Encyclopedia of an ordinary life.* New York: Broadway Books.

Russo, R. (1997). *Straight man.* New York: Random House.

Ryan, R. M., & Deci, E. L. (2000). Intrinsic and extrinsic motivations: Classic definitions and new directions. *Contemporary Educational Psychology, 25*(1), 54–67.

Shanafelt, T. D., & Noseworthy, J. H. (2017). Executive leadership and physician well-being: Nine organizational strategies to promote engagement and reduce burnout. *Mayo Clinic Proceedings, 92*(1), 129–146.

Shulman, E. P., Smith, A. R., Silva, K., Icenogle, G., Duell, N., Chein, J., & Steinberg, L. (2016). The dual systems model: Review, reappraisal, and reaffirmation. *Developmental Cognitive Neuroscience, 17,* 103–117.

Schulz, K. (2017). When things go missing. *The New Yorker, 13.*

Sibinga, E. M., Webb, L., Ghazarian, S. R., & Ellen, J. M. (2016). School-based mindfulness instruction: An RCT. *Pediatrics, 137*(1), e20152532

Singer, P. (2011). *The expanding circle: Ethics, evolution, and moral progress.* Princeton University Press.

Singer, T., & Klimecki, O.M. (2014). Empathy and compassion. *Current Biology, 24*(18), R875–R878.

60 Minutes (2018, January 10). Brain hacking [Video file]. Retrieved from https://www.youtube.com/watch?v=awAMTQZmvPE

Skiba, R. J., Horner, R. H., Chung, C. G., Rausch, M. K., May, S. L., & Tobin, T. (2011). Race is not neutral: A national investigation of African American and Latino disproportionality in school discipline. *School Psychology Review, 40*(1), 85–107.

Somerville, L. H. (2013). The teenage brain: Sensitivity to social evaluation. *Current Directions in Psychological Science, 22*(2), 121–127.

Tang, Y. Y., Hölzel, B. K., & Posner, M. I. (2015). The neuroscience of mindfulness meditation. *Nature Reviews Neuroscience, 16*(4), 213–225.

Tedeschi, R. G., & Calhoun, L. G. (2004). Posttraumatic growth: Conceptual foundations and empirical evidence. *Psychological Inquiry, 15*(1), 1–18.

Thunberg, Greta. Our house is on fire. *The Guardian* (Jan 25 2019). Retrieved from https://www.theguardian.com/environment/2019/jan/25/our-house-is-on-fire-greta-thunberg16-urges-leaders-to-act-on-climate

van Melik, B. (2018). Teaching external and internal. In A. Dews (Ed.), *Still, in the city: Creating peace of mind in the midst of urban chaos* (pp. 81–90). NewYork: Skyhorse Publishing.

Walsh, J. A., & Sattes, B. D. (2011). *Thinking through quality questioning: Deepening student engagement.* Thousand Oaks, CA: Corwin.

Verduyn, P., Lee, D. S., Park, J., Shablack, H., Orvell, A., Bayer, J., . . . & Kross, E. (2015). Passive Facebook usage undermines affective well-being: Experimental and longitudinal evidence. *Journal of Experimental Psychology: General, 144*(2), 480–488.

Weng, H. Y., Fox, A. S., Shackman, A. J., Stodola, D. E., Caldwell, J. Z., Olson, M. C., . . . & Davidson, R. J. (2013). Compassion training alters altruism and neural responses to suffering. *Psychological Science, 24*(7), 1171–1180.

Wenzlaff, R. M., & Wegner, D. M. (2000). Thought suppression. *Annual Review of Psychology, 51,* 59–91.

Wong, S. Y., Chan, J. Y., Zhang, D., Lee, E. K., & Tsoi, K. K. (2018). The safety of mindfulness-based interventions: A systematic review of randomized controlled trials. *Mindfulness, 9*(5), 1344–1357.

Yalom, I. (2010). Retrieved from https://www.psychologytoday.com/ca/blog/in-therapy/201009/yalom-the-here-and-now.

Yeager, D. S., & Dweck, C. S. (2012). Mindsets that promote resilience: When students believe that personal characteristics can be developed. *Educational Psychologist, 47*(4), 302–314.

Zeidan, F., Emerson, N. M., Farris, S. R., Ray, J. N., Jung, Y., McHaffie, J. G., & Coghill, R. C. (2015). Mindfulness meditation-based pain relief employs different neural mechanisms than placebo and sham mindfulness meditation-induced analgesia. *The Journal of Neuroscience, 35*(46), 15307–15325.

Zeidan, F., Johnson, S. K., Diamond, B. J., David, Z., & Goolkasian, P. (2010). Mindfulness meditation improves cognition: Evidence of brief mental training. *Consciousness and Cognition, 19*(2), 597–605.

FURTHER RESOURCES

PROGRAMS, COURSES, AND
RESEARCH ORGANIZATIONS

American Mindfulness Research Association
The mission of the organization is to provide a clearinghouse for mindfulness-based scientific research.

https://goamra.org/

Challenge Day
Experiential programs for communities of youth that demonstrate the possibility of love and connection through the celebration of authentic emotional expression.

https://challengeday.org

Center for Adolescent Studies
Online mindfulness courses focused on high-risk youth.

https://centerforadolescentstudies.com/

Center for Mindfulness at University of Massachusetts:
Training and research headquarters for Mindfulness-Based Stress Reduction program and work of Jon Kabat-Zinn.

https://www.umassmed.edu/cfm/

Contemplative Education and Youth Development:
Youth mentoring and training for educators working with teens and adolescents.

www.therealmansa.com

Inward Bound Mindfulness Education

Meditation retreats for teenagers that blend silent meditation practice, group work and community.

https://ibme.com/

Lineage Project

Shares mindfulness practices with young people navigating incarceration, homelessness and academic challenges.

http://www.lineageproject.org/

Mansa

Contemplative education, mentoring and youth development

http://therealmansa.com/

Middlesex School

Private school with fully integrated mindfulness program and resources for other schools.

https://www.mxschool.edu/resources-schools

Mindful Schools

Introductory and in-depth training for educators seeking to bring mindfulness into their work with youth.

https://www.mindfulschools.org/

Mindfulness Director Initiative

Community initiative supporting interested schools with qualified mindfulness directors and other resources.

https://mindfulnessdirector.org/

Spirit Rock: Teen and Family Programs

Provides daylong and residential retreats geared to youth, families and parents.

https://calendar.spiritrock.org/family-programs/

Search for Scientific Research on Mindfulness

The National Institutes of Health provides a database where you can search for scientific research, including that related to mindfulness. Summaries of the research are freely available.

https://www.ncbi.nlm.nih.gov/pubmed/

The Still Quiet Place

Courses and resources from integrative physician, Amy Saltzman.

http://www.stillq lace.com

UCLA Mindful Awareness Research Center

Center for mindfulness training and research based in UCLA's Department of Psychiatry.

https://www.uclahealth.org/marc/

COMPANION CURRICULUM:

The Mindful Schools Curriculum for Adolescents: Tools for Teaching Awareness, Oren Jay Sofer and Matthew Brensilver

RECOMMENDED READING:

Mindful Games: Sharing Mindfulness and Meditation with Children, Teens, and Families, Susan Kaiser Greenland

A Mindfulness-Based Approach to Working with High-Risk Adolescents, Sam Himelstein

The Trauma-Sensitive Classroom: Building Resilience with Compassionate Teaching, Patricia Jennings

The Way of Mindful Education, Daniel Rechtschaffen

Teaching Mindfulness Skills to Kids and Teens, Christopher Willard and, Amy Saltzman, eds.

Brainstorm: The Power and Purpose of the Teenage Brain, Dan Siegel

The Mindful Teen, Dzung X. Vo

Wide Awake, Diana Winston

MOBILE APPS:

For youth:

Breathr
   https://keltymentalhealth.ca/breathr

Stop, Breathe, & Think
   https://www.stopbreathethink.com/

For adults:

Calm
   https://www.calm.com/

Headspace
   https://www.headspace.com/

Insight Timer
   https://insighttimer.com/

Simple Habit
   https://www.simplehabit.com/

Ten Percent Happier
   https://www.tenpercent.com/

INTERVIEWS AND PERSONAL COMMUNICATION

Collazo, Enrique. September 25, 2018.

Fein, Forest. September 15, 2018.

Gillett Archer, Khalila. September 25, 2018.

Minerva, Charisse. October 8, 2018.

Morey, Jessica. September 10, 2018.

Morris, Ervin. September 11, 2018.

Smith, Dave. August 23, 2018

Speight, Jaylin. June 25, 2019.

Tamori Gibson, Jozen. August 29, 2018.

van Melik, Bart. September 12, 2018.

Worthen, Doug. September 25, 2018.

INDEX

absent adults, 39

abuse

substance, 149

accountability

radical, 121–22

active usage

passive usage *vs.*, 144

addiction(s)

distractions and, 141

adolescence. *see also* adolescent(s)

balancing authority and motivation
during, 21–22

brain changes during, 17

challenges of, 17–24

as crucial period of development,
16–17

development during, 15–27 *see
also* adolescent development;
mindfulness

forging identity during, 21

healthy eating intervention during,
22–24

identity formation and autonomy
during, 20–21

putting developmental theory into
practice during, 24–27

risk taking during, 17–19

role confusion during, 21

self-compassion during, 128,
131–33

sensitivity to social stress during,
19–20

volatility during, 17–19, 21

adolescent(s). *see also* adolescence;
adolescent development

anger in, 115–27 *see also* anger

burnout in working with, 45–49
see also burnout

cannabis use among, 149

dependence on social media, 141–46

dependence on technology, 141–46

fragility of, 154–55, 183

giving space to, 64–68

hunger for autonomy in, 116

making mindfulness relevant
for, 76–89 *see also* relevance of
mindfulness

mindfulness in development of,
15–27 *see also* adolescent development; mindfulness

mindfulness retreats for, 24–27 *see
also* mindfulness retreats

navigating pleasures and distractions, 137–51 *see also* pleasure(s);
specific types and distraction(s)

obesity among, 22–24

adolescent(s) (*continued*)
  resistance from, 95–113 *see also*
    resistance
  self-compassion among, 128,
    130–33
  self-evaluation among, 131–32
  self-harshness among, 127–36 *see*
    also self-harshness
  self-judgment among, 128
  social comparison among, 128,
    131–32
  social media platforms impact on,
    20
  stress hormone responses in, 19–20
  substance use among, 148–49
  theory of mind in, 19
  trauma and, 153–70
adolescent development
  as crucial period of development,
    16–17
  mindfulness in, 15–27
  putting developmental theory into
    practice, 24–27
adult(s)
  absent, 39
advanced technology
  in making mindfulness relevant for
    adolescents, 78–79
Adverse Childhood Experience
  Study, 156
Against the Stream Buddhist Medi-
    tation Society, 203
agency
  in making mindfulness relevant for
    adolescents, 86–88

agreement(s)
  group *see* group agreements
Ahmanson-Lovelace Brain Mapping
    Center
  at UCLA, 38–39
alliance(s)
  therapeutic, 62
American Mindfulness Research
    Association, 195
Angelou, M., 29
anger, 115–27
  calibrating appropriateness of,
    125–26
  discernment, delusion and, 122–
    23
  establishing motivation for work-
    ing with, 117–24
  exacerbation of, 126–27
  experiences of, 116–20
  expressions of, 119–20
  fueling of, 122
  honey of, 123
  investigating, 123–24
  navigating, 123–27
  radical accountability without self-
    blame, 121–22
  as "The Sheep in Wolf's Clothing,"
    119–21
Anger: Wisdom for Cooling the
    Flames, 120
Annual Review of Psychology
  on mindfulness interventions, 160
ANS. *see* autonomic nervous system
    (ANS)
Archer, K.G., 64, 105, 173

assumption(s)
  in working with resistance, 97–99
attachment(s)
  healthy, 62, 63
attention
  mindfulness-generated, 171
  as resource, 142–43
attentional control
  in mindfulness, 6
attentional stability
  in mindfulness, 5
attunement
  defined, 60
authenticity
  described, 56–57
authentic relationships
  building, 55–64
  case example, 53–54
  self-disclosure in building, 56–59
  showing genuine interest and
    empathy in building, 59–64
authority
  balancing with motivation, 21–22
autonomic nervous system (ANS),
  90–91
autonomy
  during adolescence, 20–21
  adolescents' hunger for, 116
  in making mindfulness relevant for
    adolescents, 80
avoidance
  experiential, 163
  mindfulness practice between
    entanglement and, 164
  rigid strategies of, 164

awareness
  of impermanence, 182
  maturation through, 43–44
  mindfulness practice as cultivation
    of, 30
  present-moment, 3–4
  self- *see* self-awareness
  social, 7 *see also* social and emo-
    tional learning (SEL)
"a wolf in sheep's clothing," 119

Baer, R., 160–61
balanced nonreactivity, 3–4
barrier(s)
  institutional, 111–13
  personal, 108–10
  structural, 111–13
  in teaching, 108–10
behavior(s)
  challenging *see* resistance
being grounded, 39–40
being seen
  experience of, 59–64
Black Lives Matter movement, xvi
blamelessness of feeling, 121–22
  defined, 121
Bonanno, G.A., 157
Bowlby, J., 62
brain
  adolescence effects on, 17
Brensilver, M., 203
Brontë, C., 147
Brooklyn Zen Center (BZC),
  53–54, 67, 71, 90, 94
Bryan, C.J., 22

Buddhist meditation, 203
   mindfulness from, 2
burnout
   building network in handling, 49
   compassion fatigue *vs.*, 46
   defined, 45
   handling, 45–49
   human needs protecting against, 47
   self-care in protecting against,
      46–49
   signs and symptoms of, 45
   in working with adolescents,
      45–49
BZC. *see* Brooklyn Zen Center (BZC)

cannabis use
   among adolescents, 149
care
   expanding circle of, 171–84
CASEL. *see* Collaborative for Aca-
      demic, Social, and Emotional
      Learning (CASEL)
Center for Adolescent Studies, 98,
   195
Center for Mindfulness
   at University of Massachusetts, 195
Challenge Day, 48–49, 57–58, 85,
   98–99, 195
children
   MBCT for, 170
choice
   in making mindfulness relevant for
      adolescents, 86–88
chronic pain
   mindfulness for, 1

circle of care
   expanding, 171–84
cognitive control system, 18
Collaborative for Academic, Social,
      and Emotional Learning
      (CASEL), 7, 60–61
Collazo, E., 48, 57, 60–61, 85, 98–99
Columbia University, 204
Common Core State Standards, 33
communication
   nonverbal interpersonal, 41–42
community(ies)
   in protecting against burnout, 49
compassion fatigue, 46
   burnout *vs.*, 46
concentration
   described, 5
   in kindness practices, 134–35
   in mindfulness, 5
congruence
   inner and outer, 40–43
connection(s)
   in making mindfulness relevant for
      adolescents, 81–84
consciousness
   extinguishing, 183
contagion(s)
   emotional, 38
container(s)
   creating, 68–74
   defined, 68
   described, 68–69
   group agreements in creating,
      69–73
   routines in creating, 73–74

Contemplative Education and Youth
    Development, 195
control
  attentional, 6
Copeland, W.E., 156
coping mechanisms, 137–51. *see
    also* pleasure(s); *specific types and*
    distraction(s)
coregulation
  voice prosody modulation in, 40
Cowan, M., 32
cultivation
  in kindness practices, 134
curiosity(ies)
  developmental, 139
curriculum delivery
  described, 33

Dahl, R.E., 17–19, 139
Dalai Lama, 118
Dass, R., 173
Davidson, R.J., 46
Deci, E.L., 76
decision making
  in SEL, 8
decision-making skills
  SEL in developing, 9
delusion
  discernment, anger and, 122–23
desensitization
  systematic, 165–66
development
  adolescent *see* adolescent develop-
    ment
developmental curiosities, 139

developmental theory
  in adolescent development, 24–27
dignity
  purpose and, 80
discernment
  delusion, anger and, 122–23
discomfort
  productive, 166–69
disempowerment
  in sexual relationships, 147
distraction(s)
  addictions and, 141
  mindfulness in dealing with,
    150–51
  naturalness of, 138–41
  navigating, 137–51
  sexuality as, 146–48
  sexual urges and choices among,
    146–48
  substance use, 148–49
distress
  exposure therapy for, 168–69
  psychological, 132
  self-compassion and, 132
  worrisome, 166–69
drop-out
  from mindfulness programs, 162
"dual systems model," 18
Dweck, C., 131

eating
  healthy, 22–24
education
  mindfulness in, 10–13
Ekman, P., 37

embodied teaching, 29–51
  described, 32
  establishing mindfulness practice,
    49–51
  experience in mindfulness in, 31
  finding our way, 30–33
  handling burnout, 45–49
  inner and outer congruence in,
    40–43
  maturing through awareness, 43–44
  of mindfulness, 29–51
  nervous system as intervention,
    33–36
  nonverbal information in, 36–40
  relationships in, 31
  skill sets in, 31–32
  in teaching mindfulness to adoles-
    cents, 29–51
  using one's presence to shape emo-
    tional atmosphere in, 39–40
emotion(s)
  within larger context of narrative
    history, 116–17
  in mapping incompleteness,
    128–29
  prosocial, 5
emotional atmosphere
  using one's presence in shaping,
    39–40
emotional contagion, 38
emotion regulation
  in mindfulness, 6
empathy
  defined, 60
  showing, 59–64

empowerment
  mindfulness in, 173
engagement
  group, 89–94
  social, 89–94
entanglement
  mindfulness practice between
    avoidance and, 164
equanimity
  defined, 4
  described, 4, 180–81
  in mindfulness, 3, 4
Erikson, E., 21
Ervin, M., 48, 66, 73–74, 81–83,
    86–87, 90, 92, 177
experience(s)
  anger-related, 116–20
  of being seen, 59–64
  inner, 100
  mindfulness-related, 31
  potentially traumatic, 155–58 see
    also potentially traumatic experi-
    ences (PTEs)
experiential avoidance
  defined, 163
exposure therapy, 149–50
  described, 165–66
  for distress, 168–69
  mindfulness as unsystematic,
    163–66
  mindfulness practice and, 165–
    66
  systematic, 165–66
"extractive attention economy," 143
extrinsic motivation, 76–77

Facebook, 143–44
fatigue
    compassion, 46
feedback
    being open to, 179–80
feeling(s)
    blamelessness of, 121–22
Fein, F., 62, 66
felt-sense
    defined, 37
flourishing
    mindfulness and, 7
focus
    in making mindfulness relevant for
        adolescents, 79
Fox, J.J., 144
fragility
    of adolescents, 154–55
    recognition of, 183
freeze response, 92
friendship
    in making mindfulness relevant for
        adolescents, 79

Gendlin, E., 37
genuine interest
    showing, 59–64
Gibson, J.T., 53–54, 67, 96, 130
goal(s)
    in making mindfulness relevant for
        adolescents, 86–88
    personal, 86–88
"God's-eye view" of ourselves, 179
Gonzalez, E., 174
Google, 143

grounded
    being, 39–40
group agreements
    in creating container, 69–73
    examples, 70
group engagement, 89–94

Hanh, T.N., 120
Hanson, R., 47
Hardy, J., 203
harm
    mindfulness and, 159–66
    protecting mindfulness-based pro-
        gram participants from, 160–61
Harris, T., 143–45
harshness
    self-, 127–36 see also self-harsh-
        ness
Haslam, N., 154
healthy attachment
    defined, 62
    qualities in, 63
healthy eating
    during adolescence, 22–24
heartfulness practice
    self-compassion as, 133–34
heart practice(s), 5
Heinlein, R.A., 178
hierarchy of needs
    Maslow's, 147
Himelstein, S., 69–70, 98, 102, 106
"hook"
    defined, 77
    in making mindfulness relevant for
        adolescents, 77–81

hooking up, 146
"hurt people hurt people," 93–94

Iacoboni, M., 38–39
iBme. *see* Inward Bound Mindfulness Education (iBme)
identity(ies)
   forging, 21
   social, 176–80
identity formation
   during adolescence, 20–21
If You Really Knew Me, 93
impermanence
   awareness of, 182
incentive–reward processing system, 18
incompleteness
   emotions mapping, 128–29
inner experience
   mindfully tracking, 100
inquiry(ies)
   mutual, 89–94
Insight Meditation, 24–25
Insight Meditation Society
   Spirit Rock, 203
Instagram, 143
institutional barriers, 111–13
intelligence
   in making mindfulness relevant for adolescents, 79
internal state
   in working with resistance, 99–101
interpersonal communication
   nonverbal, 41–42
intrinsic motivation, 76–77

introspection, xvi
Inward Bound Mindfulness Education (iBme), 46–47, 64, 66, 81, 105, 109, 173, 196

Jane Eyre, 147
"Jedi Mind Control," 77
Jennings, P.A., 99
Johns Hopkins School of Medicine, 158–59
judgment(s)
   positive *vs.* negative, 20

Kabat-Zinn, J., 1, 2, 195
Kaiser Permanente, 204
kindness practices
   concentrating in, 134–35
   cultivating in, 134
   metabolizing in, 135
   in mindfulness training, 133–36
   in self-harshness management, 133–36
Kross, E., 143–44

Lakoff, G., 81
learning
   through relationships, 31
limit(s)
   resetting, 105–7
Lineage Project, 196
Longfellow, H.W., 123
Lorde, A., 147
"Love and Choices," 147
low self-esteem, 130
"Lysistrata," 147

Majory Stoneman Douglas High
    School, 174
Mansa, 196
March for Our Lives, 174
Maslow, A., 147
maturation
    awareness in, 43–44
MBCT-C. *see* mindfulness-based
    cognitive therapy for children
    (MBCT-C)
MBSR. *see* mindfulness-based stress
    reduction (MBSR)
McGehee, P., 131–32
McKenna, C., 32, 36–37, 39–40,
    77–78, 90–91
McLuhan, M., 32
meaning(s)
    need for, xvii
    in protecting against burnout, 48
media
    sexuality as distraction in, 146–48
    social *see* social media
    societal pressure and, 141–46
media bombardment
    societal pressure and, 141–46
meditation(s)
    Buddhist, 2, 203
    mindfulness from, 2
    Vipassana, 203
Meditation Coalition, 203
mental health treatment
    mindfulness *vs.*, 169–70
mental hygiene
    in making mindfulness relevant for
    adolescents, 79

mental training
    in making mindfulness relevant for
    adolescents, 79
mentoring
    defined, 65–66
metabolizing
    in kindness practices, 135
metaphor(s)
    in making mindfulness relevant for
    adolescents, 78–81
#MeToo movement, 146
microexpressions, 37
microscope
    understanding and, 80
Middlesex School, 196
Mindful Awareness Research Center
    at UCLA, 197, 203
Mindful Healthcare, 204
mindfulness. *see also* mindfulness
    practice(s); mindfulness pro-
    gram(s)
    in adolescent development, 15–27
    adverse events from, 160
    attentional control in, 6
    attentional stability in, 5
    balanced nonreactivity in, 3–4
    being open to feedback in, 179–80
    from Buddhist meditation, 2
    for chronic pain, 1
    components of, 3–5
    concentration in, 5
    critiques of, 171–72
    in dealing with distractions,
    150–51
    defined, 2, 30, 164, 178

mindfulness (*continued*)
  described, 2–5
  divergences and synergy between
    SEL and, 8–10
  dosage of, 159–60
  in education, 10–13
  in empowerment, 173
  equanimity in, 3, 4
  flourishing resulting from, 7
  harm related to, 159–66
  in identifying values, 173
  mental health treatment *vs.*, 169–70
  as misunderstood, 2
  obstacles in teaching, 95–113 *see
    also* obstacle(s)
  personal practice as prerequisite
    for teaching, 49–51
  positive mind states in, 5
  as practice, 3
  present-moment awareness in, 3–4
  promise of, 1–13
  quality of attention generated in,
    171
  in relationship-building, 31
  relaxed, persistent effort in, 5
  relevance of, 75–89 *see also* rele-
    vance of mindfulness
  resembling training, 9
  resistance in teaching, 95–113 *see
    also* resistance
  SEL and, 6–10 *see also* social and
    emotional learning (SEL)
  in self-regulation, 9
  self-regulatory capacity for, 159–60
  skills and practices related to, 3, 6–7
special cautions for use with, 161–63
as state, 3
teaching, 29–51 *see also* embodied
  teaching
tools of, 100–1
as trait, 3
for trauma, 153–70 *see also* trauma
in traumatic stress management,
  158–59
in treating substance abuse, 149
in understanding self-harshness, 130
as unsystematic exposure therapy,
  163–66
uses for, 1–2
mindfulness-based cognitive therapy
  for children (MBCT-C), 170
mindfulness-based interventions
  foundations of, 32–33
mindfulness-based stress reduction
  (MBSR), 2
Mindfulness-Based Stress Reduction
  (MBSR) program, 195
Mindfulness Director Initiative, 196
mindfulness practice(s). *see also* mindfulness; mindfulness program(s)
  adverse events from, 160
  between avoidance and entangle-
    ment, 164
  being open to feedback in, 179–80
  as cultivation of awareness, 30
  described, 48
  establishing, 49–51
  experience before teaching, 31
  exposure therapy and, 165–66
  guidelines for, 171

RCTs of harm related to, 160
  special cautions for use with, 161–63
  in treating substance abuse, 149
mindfulness program(s). *see also* mind-
    fulness; mindfulness practice(s)
  drop-out from, 162
  protecting participants from harm,
    160–61
  tips for, 111–12
mindfulness retreats
  for adolescents, 24–27
  age of participants, 25
  balance supervision with choice
    and autonomy, 26
  co-create agreements on conduct,
    26–27
  highlight adolescents, 26
  invite participation, 27
  meaningful connection between
    students, 25
  silent practice in, 25
  system for adult facilitation, 25–26
mindfulness training
  kindness practices in, 133–36
Mindful Schools, 32, 36–37, 196,
    203, 204
mind state(s)
  positive, 5
Minerva, C., 81–83, 85–87
mirror neurons, 38
Monitoring the Future national
    survey, 149
Montgomery, A., 35
moral progress
  described, 181

Moreland, J., 144
Morey, J., 46–47, 66, 109
Morrison, T., 147
mortality
  wise counsel of our own, 181–84
Mother Teresa, 136
motivation
  balancing with authority, 21–22
  extrinsic, 76–77
  intrinsic, 76–77
  types of, 76–77
  for working with anger, 117–24
mourning
  in resilience, 48
muddy water
  in making mindfulness relevant for
    adolescents, 80
mutual inquiry
  defined, 89
  social engagement and, 89–94
mutual respect, 53–74
  building authentic relationships in,
    55–64
  creating container in, 68–74 *see
    also* container(s)
  giving adolescents space in, 64–68
  strategies for sharing power,
    66–68
mythology
  as tool for having conversations
    with young people, 147

National Institutes of Health, 197
need(s)
  Maslow's hierarchy of, 147

Neff, K.D., 129–32
negative judgment
    positive judgment *vs.*, 20
nervous system
    as intervention, 33–36
network
    in protecting against burnout, 49
neuron(s)
    mirror, 38
Next Step Dharma, 204
Nobel Peace Prize, 175
nonreactivity
    balanced, 3–4
    capacity of, 4
nonverbal information
    in teaching mindfulness to adoles-
        cents, 36–40
nonverbal interpersonal communica-
    tion, 41–42
Norwegian Parliament, 175
Nussbaum, M., 116, 128

obesity
    among adolescents, 22–24
obstacle(s)
    overcoming, 95–113
    personal barriers, 108–10
    structural and institutional barri-
        ers, 111–13
    sustain yourself from, 109–10
Oliver, M., 182
oppression
    in sexual relationships, 147
Ortiz, R., 158–59
"Our Future," 16

pain
    chronic, 1
Palmer, P.J., 36
parameter(s)
    resetting, 105–7
Pasari, J., 77
passive usage
    active usage *vs.*, 144
past
    remembering our, 176–80
peer(s)
    in protecting against burnout, 49
Persephone myth, 147
personal barriers
    overcoming, 108–10
    in teaching, 108–10
personal goals
    in making mindfulness relevant for
        adolescents, 86–88
personal practice, 29–51
    described, 32
    finding our way, 30–33
    handling burnout, 45–49
    inner and outer congruence in,
        40–43
    maturing through awareness, 43–44
    nervous system as intervention,
        33–36
    nonverbal information in, 36–40
    in teaching mindfulness to adoles-
        cents, 29–51
    using one's presence to shape emo-
        tional atmosphere in, 39–40
pleasure(s)
    navigating, 137–51

sexual urges and choices, 146–48
substance use, 148–49
Porges, S., 90
positive judgment
negative judgment *vs.*, 20
positive mind states
mindfulness and, 5
Posner, M., 6
potentially traumatic experiences
(PTEs), 155–58. *see also*
trauma
prevalence of, 155–56
psychological symptoms following,
157
responses to, 156–58
risk for exposure to, 156
power
strategies for sharing, 66–68
practice(s)
mindfulness as, 3
personal, 29–51 *see also* personal
practice
presence
in shaping emotional atmosphere,
39–40
present-moment awareness
described, 3–4
in mindfulness, 3–4
pressure
societal, 141–46
productive discomfort
worrisome distress *vs.*, 166–69
prosocial emotions, 5
psychological distress
self-compassion and, 132

PTEs. *see* potentially traumatic experiences (PTEs)
puppy training
in making mindfulness relevant for
adolescents, 79
purpose
dignity and, 80
Putnam, H., 179

radical accountability, 121–22
defined, 121
randomized controlled trials (RCTs)
harm related to mindfulness interventions from, 160
RCTs. *see* randomized controlled
trials (RCTs)
reactivity
described, 124
relationship(s)
building authentic, 55–64 *see also*
authentic relationships
in embodied teaching, 31
learning through, 31
mindfulness in building, 31
sexual, 147
relationship-building
mindfulness in, 31
relationship skills
in SEL, 8
relevance
establishing, 75–89 *see also* relevance of mindfulness
relevance of mindfulness, 75–89
for adolescents, 75–89
agency in, 86–88

relevance of mindfulness (*continued*)
analogies in, 78–81
being real about suffering in, 84–86
choice in, 86–88
develop repertoire of strategies in, 88–89
"hook" in, 77–81
making connections in, 81–84
personal goals in, 86–88
remembering our past, 176–80
resilience
defined, 46
human needs supporting, 47
mourning in, 48
resistance
assumptions in working with, 97–99
defined, 95
engaging, 101–5
handle your internal state in working with, 99–101
reset parameters in working with, 105–7
strategies and perspectives to working with, 97–105
from students, 95–113
working with, 95–113
resource(s), 195–99
attention as, 142–43
companion curriculum, 197
courses, 195–97
interviews, 199
mobile apps, 198
personal communication, 199
programs, 195–97

recommended reading, 197–98
research organizations, 195–97
respect
mutual, 53–74 *see also* mutual respect
retreat(s)
mindfulness, 24–27 *see also* mindfulness retreats
right(s)
self-awareness as, xvi
risk taking
during adolescence, 17–19
Rogers, F., 36
role confusion
in adolescence, 21
Rosenthal, A.K., 182
routine(s)
in creating container, 73–74
Russo, R., 21
Ryan, R.M., 76

safety
in protecting against burnout, 47–48
Saltzman, A., 197
Santayana, G., 176
satisfaction
in protecting against burnout, 47–48
Say What You Mean: A Mindful Approach to Nonviolent Communication, 204
Schulz, K., 183
Search for Scientific Research on Mindfulness, 197

SEL. *see* social and emotional learning (SEL)
self-awareness
described, 6
in mindfulness, 6
as right, xvi
in SEL, 7
self-blame
radical accountability without, 121–22
self-care
described, 47
in protecting against burnout, 46–49
self-care practices
sustain yourself in, 109–10
self-compassion
during adolescence, 128, 130–33
defined, 130–31
described, 128
as heartfulness practice, 133–34
in mindfulness training, 133–34
psychological distress and, 132
self-esteem *vs.*, 131
self-confidence
lack of, 130
self-disclosure
in building authentic relationships, 56–59
strategic, 59
self-discovery
in making mindfulness relevant for adolescents, 79–80
self-esteem
low, 130
self-compassion *vs.*, 131

self-evaluation
among adolescents, 131–32
self-harshness, 127–36
among adolescents, 127–36
kindness practices in dealing with, 133–36
mindfulness in understanding, 130
terrain of, 129–31
self-judgment
among adolescents, 128
self-management
in SEL, 7
self-regulation
developing, 35
mindfulness in developing, 9
self-regulatory capacity
for mindfulness, 159–60
sensitivity(ies)
to social stress, 19–20
sexual choices
navigating, 146–48
sexuality
as distraction in media and social media, 146–48
sexual relationships
disempowerment and oppression in, 147
sexual urges
navigating, 146–48
Shakespeare, W., 120, 138
Sibinga, E., 158–59
Singer, P., 171, 181
Sister Outsider, 147
Sisyphus, 183

sky
in making mindfulness relevant for adolescents, 80
Smith, D., 57, 66, 67, 87
Snapchat, 143
social and emotional learning (SEL), 6–10
in creating harmonious classrooms and communities, 9
in developing decision-making skills, 9
divergences and synergy between mindfulness and, 8–10
goals in, 9
mindfulness and, 6–10
programs related to see social and emotional learning (SEL) programs
relationship skills in, 8
responsible decision making in, 8
self-awareness in, 7
self-management in, 7
skills and practices related to, 7–8
social awareness in, 7
social and emotional learning (SEL) programs
mindfulness in, 9–10
outcomes of, 8
school-wide results of, 8
social awareness
in SEL, 7
social comparison
among adolescents, 128, 131–32
social engagement
mutual inquiry and, 89–94

social identity
understanding, 176–80
social media
adolescents' dependence on, 141–46
sexuality as distraction in, 146–48
social media platforms
adolescents' impact from, 20
social stress
among adolescents, 19–20
societal pressure
media bombardment and, 141–46
Socrates, xvi
Sofer, O.J., 203–4
Song of Solomon, 147
space
giving to adolescents, 64–68
Spirit Rock: Teen and Family Programs, 197
Spirit Rock Insight Meditation Society, 203
Spirit Rock Meditation Center
Teachers Council and Guiding Teachers Executive Group at, 203
Spirit Rock Teachers Council, 203
stability
attentional, 5
standing up to thoughts
in making mindfulness relevant for adolescents, 80
state(s)
mindfulness as, 3
Still, in the City, 59–60
Still Chillin', 93

Straight Man, 21
stress
  social, 19–20
  traumatic *see* trauma; traumatic
    stress
stress hormone responses
  in adolescents, 19–20
structural barriers, 111–13
substance abuse
  mindfulness in treating, 149
substance use
  among adolescents, 148–49
suffering
  being real about, 84–86
  as interdisciplinary problem, 180–81
suppression
  rigid strategies of, 164
systematic desensitization, 165–66
systematic exposure therapy, 165–66

"teach back," 83
Teachers Council and Guiding
  Teachers Executive Group
  at Spirit Rock Meditation Center,
  203
teaching
  barriers in, 108–10
  embodied, 29–51 *see also* embod-
    ied teaching
  of mindfulness to adolescents *see*
    embodied teaching; personal
    practice
  relationships in, 31
technology
  adolescents' dependence on, 141–46

in making mindfulness relevant for
  adolescents, 78–79
10% Happier, 204
The Center for Humane Technology,
  143, 145–46
The Lancet, 16
*The Mindful Schools Curriculum for
  Adolescents*, 203
"the mind is like a car," 77–78
The New Yorker, 183
theory of mind
  in adolescents, 19
The Polyvagal Theory, 90
therapeutic alliance
  between therapist and client, 62
"The Sheep in Wolf's Clothing,"
  119–21
The Still Quiet Place, 197
The Taming of the Shrew, 120
thought(s)
  standing up to, 80
Thunberg, G., xvi, 175–76
"to teach is to learn twice," 90
trait(s)
  mindfulness as, 3
trauma, 153–70. *see also* potentially
  traumatic experiences (PTEs)
  among adolescents, 153–70
  defined, 154–55
  impact of, 155–58
  mindfulness and, 153–70
  productive discomfort *vs.* wor-
    risome distress related to,
    166–69
  PTEs, 155–58

traumatic event
  defined, 154–55
traumatic experiences
  potentially, 155–58 *see also*
    potentially traumatic experiences
    (PTEs)
traumatic stress
  mindfulness in treatment of,
    158–59
"Trust No One," 73
Two Truths and a Lie game, 92–93

UCLA. *see* University of California–
  Los Angeles (UCLA)
UN Climate Change Conference,
  xvi
understanding
  microscope and, 80
University of California–Los Ange-
  les (UCLA)
  Ahmanson-Lovelace Brain Map-
    ping Center at, 38–39
  Mindful Awareness Research Cen-
    ter at, 197, 203
University of Massachusetts
  Center for Mindfulness at, 195
University of Massachusetts Medical
  Center, 1
University of Texas–Austin, 35

Valley of Lost Things, 183
value(s)
  mindfulness in identifying, 173
van Melik, B., 59–60, 73, 86, 93, 100
Verduyn, P., 144
Vipassana meditation, 203
voice prosody
  in coregulation, 40
volatility
  during adolescence, 17–19, 21
Vonk, R., 129

Wegner, D.M., 164
Wenzlaff, R.M., 164
"When Things Go Missing," 183
Whitman, W., 183
Wilson, E., 16
Wise Up, 62, 66
worrisome distress
  productive discomfort *vs.*, 166–69
Worthen, D., 96

Yalom, I., 88–89
*You Are Special: Words of Wisdom for
  All Ages from a Beloved Neighbor,*
  36
Young, S., 135
"youth choice and voice," 66
YouTube, 143

ABOUT THE AUTHORS

Matthew Brensilver, MSW, PhD, is a member of the Teachers Council and Guiding Teachers Executive Group at Spirit Rock Meditation Center. He previously served as Program Director for Mindful Schools and for more than a decade, was a core teacher at Against the Stream Buddhist Meditation Society. He lectures at UCLA's Mindful Awareness Research Center about the intersections between mindfulness and mental health. Before committing to teach meditation full-time, he spent years doing research on addiction pharmacotherapy at the UCLA Center for Behavioral and Addiction Medicine and is interested in the unfolding dialogue between mindfulness and science. Matthew is the co-author, with Oren Jay Sofer, of *The Mindful Schools Curriculum for Adolescents.*

JoAnna Hardy has been exploring and practicing multiple contemplative traditions since 1999. In 2005, her focus landed on Buddhism and Vipassana meditation, which is the foundation of most of her current teaching. JoAnna teaches adult and teen silent meditation retreats, social justice based meditation classes and workshops, and works with at-risk youth and non-at-risk youth in institutional and school settings. Helping communities and individuals that don't typically have access to traditional meditation instructions and building multicultural community is top on her list of priorities. She a founding teacher of Meditation Coalition and an empowered teacher in the Spirit Rock, Insight Meditation Society lineage.

Oren Jay Sofer has been practicing meditation since 1997. Today, he teaches meditation and communication retreats and workshops nationally. A member of the Spirit Rock Teachers Council, Oren is a Certified Trainer of Nonviolent Communication and a Somatic Experiencing Practitioner for the healing of trauma. He is the founder of Next Step Dharma, an online course integrating meditation practice into daily life, and the co-founder of Mindful Healthcare, sharing communication and resilience practices with healthcare professionals. Oren also holds a degree in Comparative Religion from Columbia University, has created mindful communication training programs for Mindful Schools, 10% Happier, and Kaiser Permanente, and is the author of *Say What You Mean: A Mindful Approach to Nonviolent Communication.*